# BOB BONDURANT ON
# HIGH PERFORMANCE DRIVING

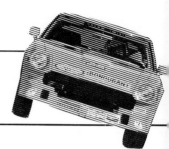

# —BOB—
# BONDURANT
# —ON—
# HIGH PERFORMANCE
# DRIVING

Bob Bondurant with John Blakemore

**Motorbooks International**
Publishers & Wholesalers Inc.
Osceola, Wisconsin 54020, USA

©1982 by Bob Bondurant and John Blakemore
ISBN: 0-87938-158-2
Library of Congress Number: 82-10624

Printed and bound in the United State of America.

Motorbooks International is a certified trademark, registered with the United States Patent Office.

1  2  3  4  5  6  7  8  9  10

Motorbooks International books are also available at discounts in bulk quantity for industrial or sales-promotional use. For details write to Marketing Manager, Motorbooks International, P.O. Box 2, Osceola, Wisconsin 54020.

Book design by William F. Kosfeld.

Front and back cover photos by John Blakemore, Berkeley, California.

Distributed in the United Kingdom by Osprey Publishing Limited, 12-14 Long Acre, London WC2E 9LP, England.

**Library of Congress Cataloging in Publication Data**
Bondurant, Bob.
  Bob Bondurant on high performance driving.
    1. Automobile racing. 2. Automobile driving
I. Blakemore, John. II. Title. III. Title:
High performance driving.
GV1029.B673 1982 796.7'2 82-10624
ISBN 0-87938-158-2 (soft)

# PHOTO CREDITS

# ACKNOWLEDGMENTS

I want to thank the following who helped make my life possible as it is today through the sport of auto racing.

My cousin, J. C. Lewis, who introduced me to sports car road racing in 1955.

Don Bechtold, for his loyalty, enthusiasm and hard work in race-preparing my #285x Indian 101 Scout in 1951 and our famous #51 orange Corvette. You helped me win the SCCA B-Production Championship and Valvoline's Best Corvette Driver of the Year in 1959!

Shelly Washburn and Bob Joehnck of Santa Barbara, who owned one of the most immaculate race-prepared Corvettes in the country. I enjoyed winning races with you both. Shelly, I want to thank you for my first pro ride.

Marie, my third wife, who gave me the encouragement and support to go professional racing with Carroll Shelby in Europe.

Carroll Shelby, for your confidence in me and for racing and test driving the famous Cobras, King Cobras and Ford GT 40's. Carroll, you gave me my real break in my professional racing career. Thank you for giving me the opportunity of working in your racing school, teaching James Garner and the others for the movie Grand Prix. That fulfilling experience is the spark that, coupled with my 150-mph accident, started the Bondurant School.

Enzo Ferrari, for my first formula ride at the U.S. Grand Prix in 1965 and a contract to drive prototypes for you in 1966.

Bernard White, for my 1966 season and first full Grand Prix ride in your two-liter BRM Formula One G.P. car.

Ken (Chopper) Tyrrell, for giving me that real driver's test at Goodwood in 1965 in your Cooper Formula Three car. I was pleased I was almost as fast as Stewart and you let me drive the Monaco Formula Three race. Thanks for teaching me how to really qualify by staying out to the last lap and running as fast as I could. It paid off as we set a new lap record, a full second faster than second place, Roy Pike. I also enjoyed driving the Formula Two Cooper, teamed with Jackie Stewart.

*Dan Gurney, for my rides in your fantastic Eagle Formula One car in both the U.S. and Mexican Grand Prix in 1966. I've enjoyed our long-term friendship. I also enjoyed training you in my school for your NASCAR ride at Riverside. What great fun!*

*Paul Newman, for sponsoring me in my Can Am rides. I'm proud to have trained you in my school for your fantastic racing career. You're great to work with!*

*Robert Wagner, I enjoyed training you and Paul for the movie,* Winning. *Remember the Lola T-70 at Elkhart Lake in turn four? I'm glad I made you drive it again, aren't you?*

*John Frankenheimer, for hiring me to work on* Grand Prix *and training James Garner, Yves Montand, Brian Bedford and Antonio Sabeto. What a great new and rewarding experience.*

*Bernard and Joanie Cahier, for all of your gracious help and thoughts throughout my entire European racing career.*

*Graham Warner of Chequered Flag Racing, London, for giving me rides early each session in Formula Three and the 427 Cobra in which David Piper and I won the Rothmans 500-mile race in the pouring rain in 1965.*

*Bobby, my son, for helping in the pits on several of my NASCAR stock car rides and IMSA races. We both like to give each other support in our racing. Congratulations on all of your wins in both the Datsun 610 in showroom stock and the orange Camaro. Let's get some more!*

*Willment Racing, outside of London, for letting me drive that Lotus Can-Am car to second at Silverstone behind Denny Hulme and winning the Formula Three race at Monza in 1966.*

*Lee Gauge, Mike Babbick, Leo Mahl and the entire Goodyear Racing staff from 1963 on. You have been a greater help than you realize. Thanks again.*

*Jackie Stewart, for all of your help in this great sport.*

*The late Graham Hill for all of his help at the Nürburgring and other tracks around the world of Formula One and to Bette Hill, his beautiful supportive wife.*

*The late Jimmy Clark, for all of his personal help and encouragement.*

*All of my employees, who have helped to make the school the number one school in the country, and a special thanks to Romy Hegarty, my partner and general manager, who helps keep me in line and make the school fantastic.*

*Many thanks to all of our Bondurant Graduates who help make the school what it is today.*

*To all of our celebrities, including Paul Newman, Robert Wagner, James Garner, Paul Williams, Clint Eastwood, James Brolin, Gene Hackman, Candice Bergen, Kent McCord, John Schneider, Bill Shatner, Fred Vryer, Kitty O'Neil, John Chancellor, James Coburn, Lee Majors, Larry Wilcox, Bruce Jenner, Robert Hays, Parker Stevenson, Tommy Lee Jones, John Frankenheimer, Christopher Cross, Craig Virgin, Ken Takakura (Japanese actor) and Yves Montand (French actor). I have enjoyed all of you and many thanks and great success to you all!*

*I especially want to thank all of the special sponsors of my school: Nissan/Datsun for their belief and continued support that makes my school possible. Bandag Retreads that last for miles and miles and give fantastic traction with smooth, predictable break-away. John & Mike's Downey Tire Centers for building all of those Bandag tires and for some great ideas. Valvoline for fourteen and one-half years of trouble-free lubrication. Quickor Suspension Systems for good-quality handling. Kontrolle gas-filled quality shocks for better handling with the Quickor setup. Fram oil filters for longer life. Autolite spark plugs for a hotter spark. Bell Helmet Company for its support and safety. Bendix for trouble-free high performance braking. Cen-*

*ter Line for strong and lightweight wheels for all of our Formula Fords. Safety Devices rollcages for the best roll cages in the industry. Race Star driving suits for safety and style. And Recaro for the best seating and car feel.*

*I want to thank the racetrack owners and managers who have helped me around the world including Riverside Raceway, Les Richter and Roy Hoard and the entire staff. Sears Point International Raceway, Jack Williams and Bobby Bowser and the entire staff. Laguna Seca, Lee Mosee and Art Glattke. Elkhart Lake, Lee Hall. Daytona International Speedway, Bill France, Sr., and Bill France, Jr., and their entire staff. As well as the Sebring Raceway with Charles Mendaz.*

*In Europe, the organizers of the famous Targa Florio and Masten Gregory, the American who taught me this circuit and how to learn all race circuits. The organizers of Goodwood, Brands Hatch and Silverstone in England. Le Mans, Reims, Rouen, Alby, Pau in France. Nürburgring, Freiburg hill climb in Germany. Monza in Italy, Spa in Belgium, Sierra Montand in Switzerland and Monaco and all of its organizers for all your help.*

*Bob Bondurant*
Sonoma, California
August 1982

I would like to thank the following people for their assistance in producing this book: Alpha Photo Products of Oakland; Eastman Kodak Company; Art Flores; Connie and John Kämpfe; Beth Kelly; Nikon Camera, Inc.; Publisher's Group West; Charlie Winton.

*John Blakemore*
Berkeley, California
August 1982

# CONTENTS

# CHAPTER ONE
## Getting Acquainted

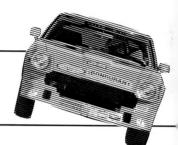

**O**ne of the most successful high performance driving schools in the world is owned and operated by Bob Bondurant. The Bob Bondurant School of High Performance Driving, which first opened its gates to students in 1968, is known in racing, corporate and law-enforcement circles as the most advanced driving school of its type. Bob's school not only teaches the aspiring racer but also the professional how to improve his driving form.

Under the close supervision of Bondurant and his staff, many novice would-be racers, famous personalities as well as some very formidable names in racing, have passed through the gates of the Bondurant School. Some take the school as a starter course, others a refresher and for some it is a "tune-up" in their driving styles. Just some of the names that Bob has given his personal instruction to are: Candice Bergen; Neil Bonnett; James Garner; Gene Hackman; Robert Hays; Rick Mears; Paul Newman; Al Unser, Jr.; Bobby Unser, Jr.; Paul Williams, just to name a few. Bob recently even had the pleasure of giving a refresher course to Dan Gurney, his old Cobra racing teammate.

Not only are Bob and his school highly respected in the racing fraternity but also in the world of street driving. In addition to providing racing instruction and high performance street driving, he also offers courses in two highly specialized areas. He has a school for instructing law-enforcement officers in the proper way to handle their police cars in nearly all situations, including pursuit. Bob also

*Dan Gurney and I had a fun two days at the school during his "refresher" course before his NASCAR comeback in 1980. . .He sure hasn't lost his touch.*

teaches what he calls his "corporate" course, one that deals with VIP's and their chauffers, teaching them how to get away from would-be terrorists and kidnappers. All of Bob's instruction deals with the how, the why and then the actual practice to ensure getting it right.

Bob's credentials are enough, in themselves, to fill a book. It is only right that we take a few quick laps through the pages that brought Bob Bondurant into the world of high performance driving instruction. About a thousand students per year attend the Bondurant School's various courses.

Bob's first interest in racing was sparked when eight years old, watching midget dirt-track racers with his father. It wasn't long until he was riding a Whizzer motorbike, and then motorcycle racing an Indian 101 Scout. Next it was hot-rodding and informal drag racing, then finally his first race car. Bob shares some of his reflections of his early days of competition; and, along with those thoughts, one can see how he has molded and formed his concepts of how to teach others to drive both faster and safer.

*The days of motorcycle racing, motocross and the ovals like the mile at Del Mar, half-mile at Bakersfield, Carroll Speedway and others brought these thoughts to mind: Motorcycle training is very, very good if you want to do car racing because you learn to race handlebar-to-handlebar, and you get used to having someone very close next to you! Most people who have not raced bikes find that in their first few years of car racing they get very nervous having someone side by side with them.*

*Here I am hot-footing it at age 18 on my Indian 101 Scout. This was at the old Carroll Speedway in Los Angeles.*

Bob's change from two wheels to four came after his cousin, J. C. Lewis, took him to the 1955 Santa Barbara road races. An entire new world opened up for him. The next year he was to drive his first race at the same circuit.

*I watched for about a year before I decided that this was what I was going to have to do. I bought a Morgan Plus-4 and ran my first race in the Saturday preliminary. I finished third. After the Saturday session, boy was it great! There was nothing to it, just go out and play like I did on the street. The great thing was there was no highway patrol to watch out for. Sunday, however, was a different tune. I only placed fourth. I was beaten by a fellow that I beat the day before. I stopped and thought to myself that there was really a lot more to it than just playing around and driving fast. From that point I got serious.*

*My first race car, the Morgan. One automobile about which you can't say, "They don't build 'em like they used to."*

*I read everything I could find about racing and driving. One of the best books was, and still is,* The Technique of Motor Racing *by Piero Taruffi. It is literally a mathematically calculated book, complete with diagrams and equations that will get nearly any driver through any turn in the world successfully, if the equations are followed and calculated correctly. Although the book was written in the fifties the concepts remain the same, even with "wing cars" and aerodynamic skirts; only the speeds in the corners have increased as the tires have better adhesion and the braking points are much later, but basically the fastest way around a turn is still the same.*

*Another book high on my list of important reading is* The Racing Driver, The Theory and Practice of Fast Driving *by Denis Jenkinson. Jenkinson's book is a classic and gives incredible insight into the make-up of a racing driver.*

*Other U.S. magazines that will help to keep you abreast of the goings-on in motoring are* Autoweek, Car and Driver, On Track, Motor Trend, *and* Road & Track; *but more about these later. Back to racing. After running the Morgan for a season, I graduated to the modified classes first with a TR-2 then anything I could get my gloves on. The next couple of years I did everything I could to improve my driving. After studying everything I could find and racing every chance I got (there's no substitute for practice), I really started to get quick, and even more important, smooth and consistent. My thoughts were now to go faster. I bought one of the cars used in the Kirk Douglas movie,* The Racers. *It was a 2.6-liter Scaglietti-bodied Ferrari. After a very short two races (and two wins) I sold it and bought my first Corvette. That was really the start of my learning to drive fast and, boy, did I enjoy it! For me there was, and still is, no substitute for horsepower. Horespower is really fun to drive. It can get you out of trouble but just the same it can get you into as much or more if you don't learn how to handle it. That 'Vette was a good one and my mechanic, Don Bachtold, was even better. I won the next eighteen out of twenty races and finished second in the other two.*

*My first real race car, at Santa Barbara in 1958. A 2.6-liter Scaglietti-bodied Ferrari that was used in the Kirk Douglas movie* The Racers.

*On my way to winning the West Coast B-Production Championship and the Valvoline Corvette Driver of the Year award. (Starting to reap the spoils of victory.)*

That gave me the 1959 West Coast B-Production championship and the Valvoline Corvette Driver of the Year award.

From then on I was driving for other people. I drove a lot of Corvettes, some modified sports cars like Max Balchowsky's Ol' Yaller and Frank Arciero's 4.5 Ferrari/Maserati and was well on my way to fame and fortune. About this time some petty politics entered the racing scene and because I competed in a race put on by one sanctioning body I was banned from the other one. All I wanted to do was race, not play politics. This sort of thing really sickened me, for political reasons they were making an example of me. They took away from me a sport that I really loved. So I said "To hell with racing!" I quit. I got both my helicopter and private pilot license and became a helicopter pilot.

I tried for a year, but I couldn't get racing out of my mind. It was really in my blood. The bad politics had passed and in 1963 Shelly Washburn approached me to drive one of the new Corvette Sting Rays. I said yes. Shortly after, Carroll Shelby talked to me about driving his yet-to-be-seen Cobra. At that time he didn't have any money and, worse yet, he still didn't even have a car done. I passed on the deal and stuck with the Corvette. As it turned out, Shelby got some help from Ford and got the Cobra on the track the same time we brought out the new Corvette. The race was Riverside and the Cobra had Billy Krause at the wheel.

It just flew! It was all we could do to keep up. From that time on, our 'Vettes had problems with this new Snake. After one more race, our fellow Corvette driver Dave MacDonald joined Shelby and then so did Ken Miles. My work was really cut out for me, just making the Sting Ray stay with them. Finally, one Sunday at

Pomona, I was the fastest. I thought finally we had it all together. But when we tried to fire the car up for the race the fuel injection packed it in. Fortunately in those days we used street parts and we took a fuel injection unit off a spectator's car. By the time we got the car together the race was two laps gone but they let me go out anyway. I chased after the pack and as it turned out I was the fastest one out there. I finished in third place.

That week I got a call from Shelby to drive in place of Ken Miles at Continental Divide Raceway as Ken had to test a new Cobra and couldn't make the race. I told Carroll I didn't know if I could even drive a Cobra. He responded, "Look here's a ticket. Be on the plane. Do you want to drive the son-of-a-bitch or not?" I drove it, thinking it was a good opportunity to find out about the competition. Well, as it happened, I won the race and stayed with the team. Then I started beating Corvettes myself.

It wasn't long after that Shelby and Ford Motor Company decided to take an American team to Europe and try to win the World Manufacturers Championship. Typically the budget was shaved slightly and although the cars and mechanics had been sent from the U.S. they decided to use American drivers who were already in Europe—Dan Gurney, Masten Gregory, Richie Ginther and Phil Hill. I made a deal with Shelby that if he paid me what he paid me in the States and covered my expenses I would move to Europe and drive the Cobra. He agreed and I left, two weeks before my first race, the Targa Florio.

I thought that I'd never learn the circuit in time, it was 44.7 miles long and over a thousand turns per lap. It was Maston Gregory who was responsible for teaching me how to learn a circuit. He taught me to first do one full lap, looking at everything, then do it section by section. I drove over each section of three or four kilometers forward and backward, studying the entire circuit for two weeks, eight hours a day, seven days a week. I had every hazard, braking point and landmark figured out. Fortunately the landmarks I picked were permanent. The Alfa Romeo team painted rocks along the track bright red to designate their various marker points. The night before the race, a practical joker (or competitor) went around the circuit and painted all their red rocks white, like the others.

Anyway, all my study paid off. For qualifying you only got one lap because the course was so long. I was the fastest qualifier until Shelby gave Gurney a second lap and he just beat me out. I was teamed with Phil Hill for this race—very astute, a fantastic driver to work with. We were leading our class when suspension failure put us out, just past the one-third point. I stayed with the team for the rest of the manufacturers championship races and we wound up a strong second to Ferrari on the season's scoreboard for 1964.

The season's highlight was winning the GT category, teamed with Dan Gurney at Le Mans. It was a fantastic feeling and wherever I'd go in Europe after that I was thought of as a Le Mans Winner. Not only did we take the GT class but a solid fourth place overall. We were in one of the Cobra Daytona coupes. It was a wonderful season but it was still a learning season, I would learn a circuit any way I possibly could. At Nürburgring the Hanseat driving school was in session and I enrolled. It worked, I became a lot faster than trying it on my own. At the end of the 1964 season was the first time that I really considered myself a true professional. The next step as far as I was concerned was Formula One.

At the end of the '64 season I got a chance to have my first taste of a Formula One car. I was testing the Ford GT 40 at Monza for John Wyer, and I was invited by Alf Francis, Stirling Moss' former mechanic, to test the ATS. I wanted to, but John Weyer said not until I had finished testing the GT 40. I finished the five days of GT 40 testing and couldn't wait for the next day's adventure. Formula One in those days was far less structured and much less professional. They didn't even use seat belts yet.

When I took the ATS out for the first time it felt a little uncomfortable at first. It was set up for Mario Cabrall, a five-foot-four-inch Grand Prix driver. My head stuck out above the roll bar and there were no seat belts! After an hour of testing I felt comfortable and confident. It was great! Now all I needed was some thinking time.

At dinner that night we were discussing who we figured had gotten through the famous Curva Grande flat out and we figured

*One of the great thrills of my life—winning the GT category at Le Mans in '64 with Dan Gurney.*

*only about six had done it at that time. It was about a 150-mph turn. Well, for the session in the morning I had resolved to myself I was going to give it a try. It took about eight laps before I did it and when I did I had a rush that was about like I swallowed my heart. I held my breath all the way through the turn. At the exit I glanced at the tach and I had come out of the turn about 300 rpm faster. I couldn't do it every lap, only once every seven or eight to start, then I got so I could do it flat out about every three or four. I just couldn't do it every lap. It was scarey! Finally I got the final "in" sign and the session was over. I thought to myself that I didn't know when I'd be in a Formula One car again at Monza so I'd try the Curva Grande just one more time, flat out.*

*There is an ancient tree on the right-hand side of the turn and its roots run under the track and cause a bump right in the racing line of the pavement. I entered that infamous turn as usual. I hit the bump, but this time the left rear half-shaft broke, the wheel flew off and the car spun to the left. I tried to spin the car back and forth to scrub off the speed. But there was only one rear wheel working and only one front wheel steering—the right one was totally off the ground because the left rear wheel was gone. No way could I save it.*

*The car took control and shot through the hedge (no Armco rails then) backward then into a ravine. I got catapulted out of the car, straight through a tree. I was wearing a plastic bubble-face shield and it was shredded off my face. I landed flat on my back on a pile of leaves. I thought I was dead. I remember flying through the hedge thinking to myself, "Shit, Bondurant, you just wrote yourself off." That was the last thing I remembered before waking up on my back. When I came to I was gasping for breath. I thought that I'd punctured a lung and broken every bone in my body. My mind flashed back to the crash, and knowing I had been flat out in sixth it had to be a horrific crash. Without trying to get up, and still gasping for breath, I tried to move things. First my toes, feet, fingers, hands, legs and arms.*

*Somehow it all worked and it was all still there, I couldn't believe it. But I was still gasping for air. The impact had knocked the wind out of me. I rolled over on my stomach, got up on my hands and knees and started looking for the car. I couldn't find it. I thought to myself, "I know I came down here in a car. Where is it?" I crawled back through the hedge, still on my hands and knees. Finally I was able to stand and found the car and when I did I realized just how lucky I really was. The real luck, in this case, was that I was not wearing a seat belt. After I was thrown out the cockpit, the car went through a tree, taking off the windshield, the top of the steering wheel, the top of the seat, the top of the roll bar and even the top of the engine. If I would have stayed with the car I would have been decapitated.*

With that experience behind me I really had long and serious thoughts if I really wanted to race Formula One or not. Fortunately the only injury I sustained was a slight back injury which was taken care of in England after five days of heat treatments, rubdowns and adjustments.

From England, I had to come directly to the States to drive one of Shelby's rear-engined King Cobras in the West Coast fall races. I really wanted to drive it badly and I didn't tell anyone about my ATS crash at Monza. Riverside was the first race and we had tire testing for Goodyear for the five days before the race. Every day on the way to the circuit I would stop and get my back worked on by a chiropractor before testing. Finally by race day I was feeling better.

Everything was looking fine. This was just the Saturday preliminary but a good finish meant a good starting position for the Sunday main event. Unfortunately it wasn't noticed until the end of the first lap that Jim Hall's Chaparral had dropped automatic transmission oil all over the starting line. Normally an oil flag is displayed a ways before the spill but this time it was right over it. The start went well—Bruce McLaren was leading, Dan Gurney was second, I was third and Walt Hansgen was right behind me. I just touched the oil with my right-side tire, started to lose it, just about got it saved and Walt tapped my left rear. Away it went! Here I was doing 100 mph plus, backward, heading for the turn-one guardrail. Looking over my shoulder I was thinking, "Holy shit! That guardrail's going to shove that engine right through

My handlebar-to-handlebar motorcycle racing was excellent experience, especially for times like this; The Monterey Grand Prix in 1964. I've got Roger Penske right in front of me, Dan Gurney immediately next door and Ed Leslie, Parnelli Jones, Bruce McLaren, Ronnie Bucknum plus a whole bunch of other guys right on my tail.

my back!" I did a quick reverse 180° spin in the other direction and tore the nose off the car instead, but it didn't hurt my back. The race was red-flagged with both oil and my car spread all over the first turn.

In those days, for the main race of the weekend, there was a catch-all race on Sunday morning for the final qualifying positions to give the nonfinishers of the Saturday heat race a chance to make the grid. My car was put back together overnight and so was Dan Gurney's and Bobby Unser's who also didn't finish the heat race. We ran the catch-all with quite a few others. Dan won, I was second and Bobby was third. This gave us forty-first, forty-second and forty-third positions on the grid.

For the main event, as they rolled my car into position I asked my mechanic if they had changed my brake pads after the qualifying race. No? They forgot! Not enough time now, maybe they'll last two-thirds the distance. They lasted just slightly longer, then it was metal-to-metal and that didn't slow things down very well. With luck I ended up fifth and the next race at Laguna Seca a good third. That season with the Cobras was a wild time, I really enjoyed it all. They were fantastic.

In 1965 I went back to Europe and drove the Cobras most of the time. At Le Mans I drove the Ford GT 40 (351 engine). I was happy, I was third-fastest qualifier. Chris Amon was fastest in a new Ford Mark 2 with a 427 engine, then John Surtees in a Ferrari, then myself ahead of Bruce McLaren in a second 427 Ford Mk 2. Behind Bruce were some more Ferraris then the rest of the Ford GT 40's. That could have been a great race but unfortunately Ford made some special "super-duper" racing heads and had them sent specially for the race. It turned out they were for the wrong engine block and the water jackets didn't line up and we were all out of the race in the first two-and-a-half or three hours. That was a shame. The GT 40 was an incredible car. I remember

An unbelievable car, the Ford GT 40. Here I am at the Mulssane Corner after qualifying third fastest at Le Mans in 1965.

*going down the Mulsanne straight in qualifying at 212 mph. I got so I could do the kink near the end of the straight without lifting, then brake hard for the 45-mph Mulsanne corner. Incredible! That car worked so super it was unbelievable. A fantastic car to drive!*

Nineteen-sixty-five was a fantastic year for Bob, he drove Formula Three for Ken Tyrrell where he set the fastest lap at Monaco (a new Formula Three record then) and drove the Cobras in the World Manufacturers Championship. Bob co-drove to win the coveted GT class in eight of ten races to give a very happy Carroll Shelby and Ford the much sought after World Manufacturers Championship title over the factory Ferrari team.

All that was left for Bob now was another shot at Formula One. That wasn't far off. Ferrari give Bob a contract to drive their sports cars in the manufacturers races for the following year and a works Formula One for the 1965 U.S. Grand Prix at Watkins Glen in October.

*Not a bad team for my first Formula One race. The best part about it was the team and the car. They were really top-of-the-line, the best. The worst thing about the race was the weather. It was horrible. Rain. Most of the race I ran about sixth, while doing so I couldn't help thinking, "Not too bad." But it got worse. The heavy rain stretched the elastic band on my goggles (there weren't*

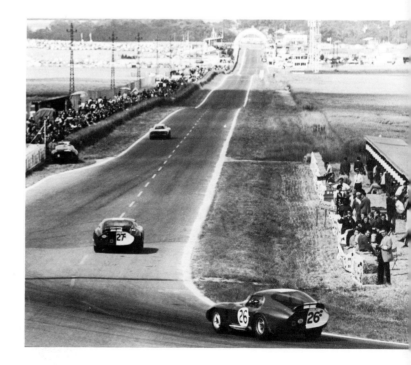

*I'm at the wheel of the Daytona Cobra #26, about to lap one of my teammates. This was Reims and here we clinched the 1965 World Manufacturers Championship, finally beating Ferrari.*

*Formula One, at last. My first F1 race and for Ferrari too! This was taken in practice at "the Glen" before my old goggles started to slip.*

full face helmets then) and they kept falling down. If they had been new they would have been ok but they were old and so were the extra pair I had in my pit so it wouldn't help to stop to change them. I kept on with one hand holding the goggles in place and the other driving. When shifting or in a corner I would put my face into the wind so that would hold them on. Not a very good end to my first Formula One race. I finished up in ninth position in a race that I should have done much better had it not been for an old but necessary piece of equipment that I took for granted.

Driving sports cars for Ferrari was rewarding but it was the other things that happened in 1966 that made it a year to look back on with good memories. Formula One was to be the direction for my season. Everything just fell into place. In 1964 I had done some driving instruction at Carroll Shelby's racing school and in '65 after the season was over I was at Riverside testing. John Timanus, who was then instructing at Shelby's school told me that John Frankenheimer was looking for some people to drive in a film he was going to do about Grand Prix racing. Frankenheimer and I met and he asked me if I would like to drive in his film. I replied, "Sure, but not if it's going to be some Mickey Mouse racing film." He exploded! "It's going to be the best damn film you ever saw!"

I was testing the new GT-350 Mustangs a couple of days later at Willow Springs and Frankenheimer came along. He was asking me all sorts of different questions about what I'd do if this happened or that happened and one of the questions was what would I do if I went off the road. The first thing, I told him, was to turn the wheel straight so that a wheel wouldn't dig in the dirt and roll the car. All through the day while riding with me he kept asking all sorts of questions. Nearing the end of the day I was moving along about 110 or 115 coming through turn nine. Wind was blowing sand across the track and the car's drift angle was increasing. I realized we weren't going to make it through the turn. I was busy driving the car off the road, turning the wheel straight and charging through sage brush and sand and I hadn't given Frankenheimer a second thought. Finally we slowed and stopped. I asked him if he was ok. He didn't say a word for a few seconds. "You all right, John?" He yells, "That was fantastic! You did exactly what you said you'd do. That's really fantastic." I asked him if he wanted to get out and watch but no, he kept riding with me. I really respect him for that. It wasn't till almost a year later, at the end of the movie Grand Prix, that I told him that my going off the road wasn't on purpose.

Despite, or perhaps because of, going off the road Frankenheimer hired me as technical consultant for his film Grand Prix. I did a little bit of everything. I drove the camera cars, the race cars in the racing scenes. It was great. I drove just about every day in a single seater. As I look back on it now probably the best thing that I did was to teach the actors in the film how to drive. Not just the stars but also John Stephens, the director of photography, and the film editor too. I taught James Garner, Yves Montand, Brian Bedford and Antonio Sabato. This teaching, little did I know then, was just a start.

Some of the driving crew from Grand Prix. Left to right are: Graham Hill, Jochen Rindt, James Garner, Guy Ligier, Dan Gurney, Jo Schlesser, Bruce McLaren, Antonio Sabato and Jo Siffert.

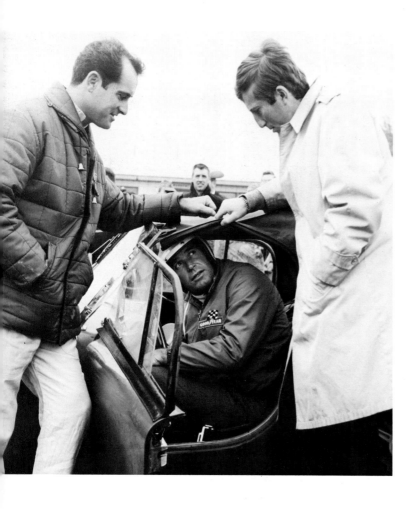

James Garner, my "star" pupil for the movie Grand Prix, was a tight fit in a 289 Cobra. Jochen Rindt and I give him some pointers before he does a hot lap at Watkins Glen.

Because of working in the film, I was able to drive every Grand Prix circuit for about two weeks before the Formula One race then for about another two weeks after it. This all worked well for me because by the first race of the 1966 season I had a Formula One drive.

Sixty-six was the year of change in Formula One, moving from 1.5-liter to three-liter engines in one big jump. This meant all the cars had to be new and the engines were sure to not be all fully developed until mid-season. While awaiting the three-liter engines, many of the teams were forced to use two-liter engines in the interim.

I drove for a private entrant, Bernard White. His team was one of those with the two-liter cars. Bernard had a two-liter BRM that was built for the Tasman series as a spare car for Jackie Stewart and Graham Hill on the works BRM team. We also used the car for filming in the movie.

*At the wheel of the two-liter BRM at Brands Hatch during my 1966 Formula One season.*

In the early part of the season it was quite conpetitive with the factory teams but, as anticipated, by mid-season the works teams started getting it right and we were quickly left behind. The first race at Monaco, one of my favorite circuits, was also the best finish of my Formula One career. I managed a fourth place behind John Surtees in a Ferrari, Stewart and Hill, both in two-liter BRM's. But from there the season got worse. The team was on a very minimal budget, the preparation of the car was nearly non-existent and finally I quit.

At the U.S. Grand Prix I drove for Dan Gurney in his four-cylinder Eagle and wound up the season in his V-12 Eagle at Mexico City.

With no hot prospects for a first-rate Formula One ride for the 1967 season I decided to stay in the U.S. and see what was available rather than take another shot at a poorly prepared "also-ran" Formula One team. There was, in the U.S., a lot of interest in the United States Road Racing Championship and the Can-Am series (Canadian-American Challenge Series).

Each of these series used the same cars, Group 7 sports racers with big engines and lots of horsepower. This caught my interest. Peter Revson liked the looks of the series too and we teamed together for the Dana Chevrolet team. Peyton Cramer ran the team and we were to get new Lola T-70's (that would have been the hot number to have). But we wound up with McLaren Mk II's and they were dogs. Not at all competitive or reliable, compared with the Lolas or Chaparrals. Peter and I drove our asses off at the Riverside opener and only placed third and fourth. That was our best race of the season. It seemed like some little thing or another was forever breaking.

That's what happened at Watkins Glen. Only it wasn't something little, it was a big one! I was traveling at about 150 mph, coming out of a corner onto the top straight, when a steering arm broke. The McLaren steered itself and shot straight toward a dirt embankment and I could see a bad one coming. It's funny what you think about in a split second. First I shut down the fuel pumps so I wouldn't burn. Then shut off the engine (I didn't want to blow it up). Then just prior to impact I thought the car was steering itself so I didn't need to hold the wheel tight; because if I did, I was going to really break up my arms and upper body. So, I took a deep breath and tried to relax. When I hit the banking the car was launched in the air and as it took off, the bank peeled the aluminum floor pan back clear to the rear bulkhead. McLarens didn't have any cross tubes in the cockpit so my feet fell out the bottom. The car rolled end-over-end then rolled sideways eight times before coming to a stop. Every time it rolled my dangling feet and legs were smashed. But I was fortunate and only ended up with a shattered right heel, two broken ankles, some broken ribs, a chip out of a vertebra and a chunk out of my forehead. But, now the bad news, I was instantly out of the racing business and in the hospital.

The second day I was in the hospital I got a yellow-lined pad and a pen and started to plan something that I had been thinking about for a long time. Since helping out Shelby in his racing school and after training the actors and crew for the movie Grand Prix I had been thinking that someday I'd like to have a driving school. I planned, on paper, a high performance driving school.

While in Europe I tried some of the different schools and worked with Jim Russell in order to use his facilities to train the people in Grand Prix. This looked like the right time to give this a try. The first experiences I had training people at Shelby's were fantastic. I really loved it. It's a super neat feeling that you get watching them get better and faster from what you have taught

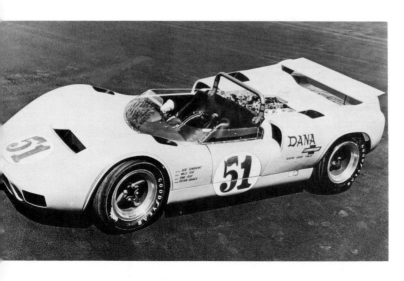

This is the McLaren MkII that helped me get into the driving school business, after it almost killed me.

them. *James Garner was a perfect example. For the movie* Grand Prix *he did a fantastic job of driving real Formula One cars. I started him out at Willow Springs Raceway in a GT-350 Mustang then put him in a Cobra 289, then a Lotus Formula Ford then finally into a Lotus Tasman Formula One car. He did fantastic!*

*Many of these thoughts crossed my mind when I was in the hospital, so I worked out a plan of how to put it all together and start a school.*

*As I got closer and closer to being well my mind was more intent on going racing again and the school idea took a back seat. I formed a company with Don Rabbitt, former Shelby P.R. man; Dick Guldstrand, driver and mechanic; and Sandy Sandine, engineer. We called it the American International Racing Corporation and we had our sights set on building a turbine car to run the FIA endurance races at Daytona, Sebring and Le Mans. We were all set to go, sponsors and all, when the FIA changed the rules from an unlimited displacement to a three-liter-engine displacement which would have made the turbine car noncompetitive. So we got two Corvettes, but the other partners were each wanting something other than the original agreement so I resigned. The*

*On my feet again after my Watkins Glen accident, proudly displaying my first fleet of instruction vehicles. This was at the Orange County International Raceway.*

27

One of my earliest jobs with the school was technical advisor and camera car driver for the movie Winning. Here I am at Indy driving the Lola T-70 camera car that we designed and built.

time had come to start my driving school. I pulled out my hospital notes and went from there.

Out of necessity the step-by-step program that I put together in the hospital called for everything to be sponsored with the exception of the rent. That was the only way I would be able to start. I put together a presentation for all my potential sponsors and I got most of them.

I reached a deal with Datsun and opened my school on the fourteenth of February 1968 at Orange County Raceway near Los Angeles. For starters Datsun gave me one 510 sedan, one 1600 roadster and one 2000 roadster. I had a Formula Vee kit car that was a couple years old, and that rounded out my fleet.

Two of the first Bondurant School graduates, Robert Wagner and Paul Newman. I trained them to drive for the movie Winning.

*Datsun's help and support over the years has been invaluable. They along with my other sponsors have made it possible to do the school in a first-class fashion, which is the only way I would have done it. Those first cars worked so well it was unbelievable. The Datsuns that I now use in the school are even much better than the first ones. I use the 810 sedans with 240Z motors and the new ZX's. The Formula Vee has long since given way to Crosley Formula Fords.*

*I stayed at Orange County for two-and-a-half years until the new Ontario Motor Speedway opened nearby. Ontario was a beautiful facility but always burdened financially. I was at Ontario for three years then their burden became mine and before it was demolished they raised the rent way out of reach. It was either close or move. Some choice. I moved to my present location at Sears Point International Raceway in the Sonoma wine country not far from San Francisco. Sears is a fantastic circuit, a real drivers' course with lots of up-hill and down-hill, much better than Ontario was. Sears is wonderful for training and instruction—like a miniature Nüburgring. I entertain no thoughts of moving the school again.*

Bob's high performance driving school has become the standard by which all the others are judged. It has blossomed into a school that is recognized and respected internationally. The programs that Bob offers are of great variety. There is a one-day advanced highway driving class with skid school, a two- and three-day high performance class and a four-day grand prix competition road race class that gives you everything from sedans, sports cars, through Formula Fords. In addition to the programmed classes Bob offers specially tailored in-

*As I said before, I like driving lots of horsepower and Dick Barbour's Twin Turbo 935 Porsche really moved . . .This was Sears Point in 1979.*

*Typical "corporate" course passengers and vehicle, driven by instructor Ron Southern.*

struction for the racer in an advanced program to dial him in to what he or she and the car are capable of doing.

In recent years there has also been the addition of the Bondurant Law Enforcement Academy for police and sheriffs and the one he calls his "corporate chauffers course," which teaches how to get away from potential kidnappers and assassins. He also offers a stunt driving course for the movies.

*Among the wide variety of cars I've enjoyed driving was this quarter-mile dirt track sprint car. I'm just hot lapping to see what it's like. . .It's great!*

No matter how specialized the area of training that is required, the Bob Bondurant school has or will make the facilities available for nearly any form of driving instruction.

Since the opening of Bob's school, racing has perhaps taken a back seat to instruction but Bob is by no means retired. He keeps his helmet and gloves ready to take to the wheel in competition any time he has the opportunity. By the time the school opened he was ready for racing again and jumped right back into Can-Am, Formula 5000, endurance racing, IMSA-prepared 935 Turbo Porsches, sprint cars and Grand National stock cars. There is no end in sight to Bob's competition career. His feelings are clear when he speaks of racing.

*I still do race from time to time for several reasons. First and foremost, I love to race. It's fun, exciting, challenging, and keeps the adrenaline flowing and for me the only thing that comes close to it is sex. From a more practical view, I also race to keep abreast of what is going on with contemporary cars. I try to race current cars that are competitive in their classes so that I can work that into my training programs. Many of my teaching staff, most of whom have been with me for many years (seven, eight, nine and longer), race presently and in a wide variety of cars. Ron Southern is an SCCA club racer now; Bill Cooper has done Le Mans and finds rides in Trans-Am; and Bob Earl, who has been with me the longest, recently won the Macau Grand Prix for Formula Atlantic cars against some of the world's leading drivers. Steve Cook has raced Daytona and Sebring as well as SCCA club races. Ron Nelson and Dominic Dobson also race Formula cars. Not only are*

*I was the fastest qualifier and set a new lap record in this 1980 Buick at Sears Point. I wound up second at the checker in this NASCAR race.*

*my instructors good competitors but more important to the learning process, they are good instructors and can communicate what they have to teach to their students.*

Although there is no substitute for actual behind-the-wheel training, proper driving technique is also arrived at through instruction, thinking and practice. The goal of this book is to give the reader the insight and instruction to come to terms with self as well as with the car. Although reading and studying is just the first step to actualizing a technique, this study helps to form the basics. Practice and utilization will in fact make you a better driver but it is very important to make use of the basics and proven methods to arrive at a full high performance potential.

A high performance driver is one who drives, not only to the full capabilities of the car but also to the capabilities of oneself.

*One of my best "students"—Gypsy Bondurant.*

# CHAPTER TWO
## Getting To Know The Lingo

*T*he following pages introduce you to the world of high performance driving. By picking up this book you have taken the first steps to improving your driving ability and, at the same time, your driving pleasure.

Before we get into the hows and whys, it is important to briefly define a few terms that are used regularly throughout the text. To many these words are already familiar but to others they may create some confusion as to what they really mean. Each will be dealt with in a later chapter of the book but here is a starter of brief explanations to get you going. All these terms relate to cornering and to traction.

*Oversteer:*

When you have adhesion and traction with the front wheels of the car, but the rear wheels lose traction and slide toward the front. It is also referred to as being "loose" or "coming-around-on-you." The oversteer can be to either the left or to the right and its effect decreases the radius of the turn.

*An example of oversteering with one of my school Formula Fords in a right-hand turn.*

*Here I am leading Pedro Rodriguez at Riverside. Pedro's Ferrari is very "loose"—a good example of oversteer.*

*Understeer:*

When you have traction with the rear wheels but the front wheels lose traction and, regardless of the steering correction, the front of the car slides to the outside of a turn. Understeer increases the radius of the turn. It is also referred to as "pushing" or "plowing."

*See how the front wheels of the Formula Ford are pushing to the outside of the turn in this example of understeer.*

*A good example of a little low-speed understeer. This is the Gurney Eagle Weslake V-12 Formula One car in the hairpin at the Mexico City Grand Prix in 1966.*

*Line:*

This refers to the physical line of movement that a car takes through any given turn from entry, to apex, to exit. A line can be either good or bad, right or wrong.

*Just like a train, notice how all five of these Can-Am cars are following me through pretty much the same line in the "Corkscrew" at Laguna Seca in 1970.*

*Apex:*

The driving apex of a corner is the *area of a corner,* not just a clipping point, where the inside front wheel runs closest to the inside of a given corner. Where you apex is directly related to how you entered the turn and will affect how you exit the turn. An apex area varies from corner to corner and, for example, can be too early or too late.

*Mike Parkes is right behind my Tim Parnell Team Brabham on the proper line in the apex area of this turn at Reims. I seem to be a little too wide. . .it was my first Formula Two race.*

*Trail-Brake:*

After the major braking has been completed for a corner, trail-braking is, essentially, just riding the brake into the first third of the corner, gradually releasing the pressure and smoothly switching from brake to throttle. By trail-braking you maintain a forward-directed weight transfer and down force on the outside front wheel, increasing its tire patch area which gives better steering control.

*Tire Patch:*

A tire patch is the area on the bottom of the tire that is in direct contact with the road. The tire patch can vary in size and shape with the tire type, size, kind of car, the attitude of the car on the road, the suspension and also whether entering or exiting a turn. Depending on the transfer of weight of the car, acceleration or braking or turning, one tire can have a different tire patch or contact area than the other three. Tire patch varies constantly. Ideally one wants the maximum tire patch possible in contact with the road. Trail-braking helps to control the tire patches of all four tires.

*Like in downhill ski racing, being airborne looks impressive, but in order to corner, brake and go fast you want maximum contact with the road surface. I was driving this factory Porsche Carrera at the Nürburgring, 1966. Being ariborne is just a part of going fast here.*

*Drifting:*

Drifting is or should be a controlled function. It is directly opposed to sliding or skidding which are out-of-control conditions. Drifting is a balance. The rear of the car can drift with throttle control as can the front. The optimum condition one wants to create is an evenness that permits the entire car, front and rear, to drift in a balanced lateral motion on the border of maximum traction. This drifting effect utilizes gravity forces (inertia forces) on all aspects of the car, allowing it to travel its fastest at a speed just past the absolute limit of adhesion.

Assuming that you have come to terms with these terms the rest of the text should be a little easier to understand, and make for more pleasurable reading. Reading, like driving, should be enjoyable, not just hard work, so we'll try to keep it light and informative.

*A typical Corvette four-wheel drift; This was in 1960—it's the same today only at faster speeds. (Look how skinny the tires were then.)*

*Here's Al Unser, Jr., practicing what I taught him. It takes a lot of practice to avoid being out of control in a slide or skid. Just about the point of no return on our skid pad, but he caught this one.*

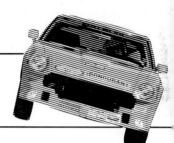

# CHAPTER THREE
# *Getting Comfortable*

**O**ne of the most important basics in driving any car, and usually one that's the most overlooked is, clearly and simply, *comfort*. If you aren't comfortable in the car you will not enjoy driving it as much, nor will you drive it as well. When we say comfortable we don't mean driving from an over-stuffed lounge chair. That deadens sensitivity, we want to *maximize sensitivity*. It is important to sit properly so that you can easily operate all of the controls and so your body can *feel* what the car is doing under it.

The essence of high performance driving, be it on the street or on the racetrack, is to control weight transfer, in order to achieve maximum traction during the basic functions of braking, cornering and acceleration. And to have that control you must be seated properly.

All of your sources of input give you the ability to control your car but the two major things that affect your performance are, *what you see* and *what your body feels*. Everything that the car does is transmitted right back to you through the seat, steering wheel and foot pedals. The ideal driving position is one that allows your body to maximize the input that is available to it. The optimum seating position is one that has as much of your body as possible in contact with the seat.

You should have your buttocks tucked well into the crotch of the seat so you can feel what the car is doing with your fanny, the back of

*The proper seating position. Arms bent, seated upright with fanny tucked into crotch of the seat. Legs should be slightly bent too. Shoulder harness is snug.*

your legs and your back. You should be sitting as upright as possible because it helps to make you more alert. When driving a formula racing car or sports racer it is of course impossible to sit upright—they are designed almost strictly for aerodynamics and the seating is dictated by the design. Whereas a production racer or street car is designed with a different purpose in mind and it is possible to modify the car so that you are able to sit in the best possible position.

*Dan Gurney was the one who taught me the importance of a proper seating position. I remember, in the fifties, when we were both racing Corvettes. I was bombing along, all slouched over and hanging on just bouncing all around inside the car. Dan was "bolt-upright." He never seemed to move. He was like a statue someone had put in the driver's seat. He taught me, I listened and he was right.*

*Sitting upright is where it all begins. The seats of modern production cars are a much better fit than the old bench type of yesterday but even so, you might want to replace the stock seat with a unit such as a Recaro adjustable one.*

The seat should be adjusted so that you have a bent-arm driving position, and the controls fall into easy reach. Distance from the seat to the steering wheel is really important and the extremes should be avoided. The first World Champion, Giuseppi Farina drove in the straight-arm style. He sat so far back from the wheel that his arms were unbent and most of the steering had to be done with the shoulders. It is not only a fatiguing way to drive but also a less precise way.

The other extreme would be Richard Petty driving NASCAR (National Association for Stock Car Automobile Racing) Grand National stock cars. Richard practically sits right on top of the steering wheel. For the NASCAR ovals it's all right but if you have to react quickly in a street or road racing situation you won't have enough room to move freely.

The best position is one somewhere between the two. Find a position that is a comfortable distance from the wheel with your elbows bent at an angle of about 120 to 140 degrees. In a street car if your seating position is poor then you will become more easily fatigued, less alert and more likely to fall asleep at the wheel on a long trip. In a racing car you simply won't be as fast, consistent or smooth. Combine that with early fatigue and you won't do too well.

*In 1971, at the start of the Can-Am season, I was driving for the Paul Newman-sponsored team with Lothar Motschenbacher. We had brand new McLarens (this was the right car to have that season). His car was delivered first and it was all completed before mine had even arrived. When mine came, it was loaded on the transporter and was literally put together in the transporter on the way to the first race, at Mosport. The car was finally finished at the track and my dialing-in time was just a few laps. I had twenty minutes in the car to do a shake-down, qualify, feel what the car was doing and figure what the suspension and brake bias changes had to be. What I didn't realize was that we hadn't padded the seat at all. I was so intent on getting the car sorted out right and qualifying that I completely overlooked the seating compartment.*

*Here's that nice McLaren that exhausted me at Mosport. I can't emphasize too much the importance of good comfort and proper seating to help you drive up to your car's maximum potential.*

Note the extra padding we've placed on
the Datsun's seat to provide a better fit
for singer, song writer and actor Paul
Williams; one of my most loyal students.

*As it was, Lothar and I turned identical times for third and
fourth fastest on the grid. Even at the start of the race I still didn't
realize that we hadn't adjusted my seat (the only way the seat of a
Can-Am car was adjusted was by padding). About a third of the
way through the race I was starting to get tired—I was in great
shape then and used to driving long distances. The problem was, I
was sitting too far back from the wheel and my arms were at full
length to steer the car through the corners. So I was steering with
my wrists and my shoulders instead of my forearm and biceps, as I
would be in a normal bent-arm driving position, where I had
more power and strength. So, as my arms got more tired, I would
pull myself forward in the seat with the steering wheel, up to a
bent-arm position, and drive five or six laps flat out then I'd relax
my arms for a few laps and then do the sequence again. At the end
of the race I was exhausted. I finished fourth but I know that if
my seating position had been normal I would have been able to at
least finish second or third as the car was working wonderfully.*

To maximize the way your body fits the seat, and have it make
proper contact, you must also take into consideration your seat belt
shoulder harness and submarine belt or crawl strap. In racing the
importance of tight seat belts can't be stressed too much. If your belt
or harness is at all loose the forces of cornering and braking will cause

you to slide in the seat. This also applies to street driving. The way cars are built today you are best off using your belts.

If you have an open car and are concerned about being strapped in during a roll-over, then install a roll bar. Racing cars, open or closed, have roll-over protection as a mandatory rule for safety. If you think that you might need it with your driving technique on the street then don't take a chance, put one in. Open car or closed, safe is sane. Roll bars also tend to stiffen the chassis of a car making it handle better thus sending more input right to the driver's seat.

Seat belts are like roll bars, optional to use for the street, but mandatory for racing. If you use them make sure they are snug. Sliding around in the seat is distracting and doesn't let you read the input coming from the car properly. Another simple reason for strapping the belts tight is that most nylon belts stretch. If you happen to roll the car and your belt is not tight you'll probably hit your head on the roof, or worse if it's an open car.

Shoulder harnesses also help drivers avoid leaning their bodies into the turns. Remember Gurney in the Corvette, "Like a statue!" If you have to lean into a turn then you are reducing the contact area of your back to the seat, thereby reducing the input area for the car to tell you what is going on. Leaning also increases your fatigue rate and slightly alters your visual perspective. If you feel that you have to lean to offset the g forces because your car corners so well, or perhaps your suspension is so soft you can't see out of the window if you don't, then try just tilting your head, not your whole upper body.

*One way to counteract cornering forces is by tilting your head into the corner, but keep as much of you as possible in contact with the seat. This is the Freiburg Hill Climb where I took first place with the Cobra in 1964.*

Now that you know how to sit in your car it's time to get your hands on something meaningful. . .the steering wheel. Don't forget, your tires, the wheels and suspension are sending input up the steering column and right out the spokes to the rim of the steering wheel to your hands. So, first the steering wheel should be gripped firmly, but not too tight. No "white-knuckle-driving" please. Relax into a firm grip but don't strangle it. If you grip the wheel too tightly you will fatigue yourself and your tense muscles will cause you to make small, involuntary movements of the wheel if you are driving really hard. If you find your grip tightening just take a deep breath. That will relax your shoulders and arms—and your whole upper body will feel better.

Now that you've relaxed your strangle-hold on this little twelve-inch wheel that's going to corner five-hundred horsepower of fury, you'd better know where to put those hands to make it all work right. Think of the wheel as the face of a round clock, picture where three o'clock is, put your right hand there. Fine, now picture where nine o'clock is and put your left hand there. This is what is referred to as the three-and-nine hand position. If you have a three-spoke wheel on your car, chances are that the spokes run at three, six and nine o'clock. (There are some variations but that's another story.) If your family sedan's wheel is too big and has just one bar across it (and your hands keep slipping on the plastic) I'd recommend that you get an aftermarket steering wheel that's padded and covered in leather or vinyl to make it less slippery. There are many available, the ones

*The three-and-nine position. Notice the way my thumbs rest on the short padded sections in the BMW road car.*

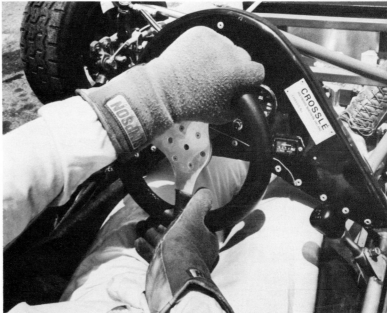

*Now make a turn keeping your hands in the same location on the wheel.*

used at the Bondurant school are produced by Momo of Italy, and can be purchased through the school. It is really a worthwhile investment for your car.

Now, with your hands at three and nine o'clock try to make a turn keeping your hands there without moving all over the wheel. If you grip the wheel at three and nine and hook your thumbs over the tops of the spokes, lightly resting on them, then you have created one more source of input—the vibration of the steering wheel spokes. Your thumbs resting on the spokes also give you just that extra little bit of feel and leverage in hard cornering. By always gripping the wheel at the same position you will always know just how much steering you have put in and, even more importantly, you know just where straight ahead is. Knowing where straight ahead is doesn't seem that important when you are heading down a straight-away but when you're in a turn out of shape or you just lost it, that instinct can mean a lot.

Back to input. . .Another very good reason for keeping your hands in one place is that the more you move them around the less time they are in contact with the steering wheel, losing the advantage of chassis information being fed in. Remember to feel what the car is doing through the steering wheel at all times.

If you need more steering wheel input to get around a sharp or tight corner, then slide the inside hand up to the 11 o'clock position on the right-hand turn keeping the left hand at 9 o'clock, so that the left hand can smoothly and precisely steer the car out of the corner. Do just the opposite on a left-hand corner, sliding the left hand up to the 1 o'clock position. This is important for precise cornering. If the wheel requires more input (as in a car with slower turning rates),

*Final preparations before taking some laps—we're making the seat nice and comfortable. An excellent time to adjust your mirrors; especially with a willing assistant handy.*

then do a hand over position using the thumbs under the opposite side spokes.

The kind, size and shape of the steering wheel is up to you but don't get a rim so thick or thin that it makes it difficult to get a good grip on it. The size and thickness of the wheel are very important for *car feel.*

*I like the leather-covered wheel that has the padding coming down onto the spokes so I can put my thumbs on top comfortably. On the Cobras I used to tape sponge rubber there for padding. The bare steel spokes would tear my thumbs up. When I did Sebring, Daytona, Le Mans—all the long distance races—I used to have rubber taped to the spoke where it met the wheel. It was crude but it's a lot better than chewing up your thumbs.*

Now that you've got your five-hundred-horsepower baby wheeling along, let's look around, what can you see? Can you see the Highway Patrol in your rearview, or in your right-side mirror, or for that matter in your left one? No? How do you know where he is? You have to know what is going on around you—both on the track and on the street. Mirrors are there as a driving aid. Use them. To be able to use them they must be adjusted properly. Take the time to do it. If you are in a racing car it'll save a lot of time and aggravation to get them adjusted before you fasten your seat belts. because chances are you won't be able to reach them afterward. They are a lot easier to adjust on your street car so don't just forget or say that they are almost ok,

*Just a quick glance in the mirror lets you know what's going on behind you—with a driver like Graham Hill on your tail, you'd better put the willy to it!*

even though you have to lean clear across the car to see out of the right one. Adjust them and keep them clean. Dirty mirrors are a serious cause of night glare.

Some racers don't use their mirrors and some racers crash into cars trying to overtake them; but keep your eyes fixed on them or you'll be in trouble too!

*A student of mine recently was so intent on watching this other student (very fast and very advanced) come up on him that he ran straight off the road. He was looking at him in his mirror, not at the up-coming turn.*

*Pay attention to what is in front of you but use your mirrors to tell you what to expect from behind. Adjusting your mirrors may be the last thing that you do before starting your car, but do it, and use them.*

Now that you're seated properly and have your hands correctly placed with your belt snug and your mirrors adjusted, do you feel in control? Almost? Maybe after the next chapter.

# CHAPTER FOUR

# *Getting To Know The Controls*

**N**ow you've learned the importance of feeling the input from the car to you. This can't be over-emphasized. But, there is another bit of input, the significance of which can't be stressed enough either: the input *from you,* the driver, *to the car.*

You're all strapped in and comfortable. But before you touch that key you need to know what your hands and feet should be doing.

While your hands are resting at three and nine let's put your feet to work. Important Step Number One: Make sure they reach the pedals, *comfortably.* This can be accomplished by adjusting the seat properly for bent leg and bent arm position at the wheel. If your feet still don't reach the pedals, you can fix the pedals. A plate can be welded, pop-riveted or bolted onto the pedals to move them closer to you or with many cars there is room to remount the whole pedal assembly closer or farther away. As with the distance from the seat to the steering wheel, the distance from the seat to the pedals is crucial.

Like your bent-arm driving position you want to have a bent-leg driving position. You want to be able to reach the pedals with the balls of your feet, *not your toes.* Never have your legs so straight that you have to stretch to work the pedals with the tips of your toes. You should be positioned so that when you have the brakes or clutch fully depressed, you still have your knees bent. What if your leg was fully extended when the brakes were on full and the pedal level dropped or the brakes started to fade during a real heated drive? You'd really be in trouble. The same goes for the throttle. If the cable stretches

*The bent-leg driving position helps assure your ability to comfortably work all the pedals with the balls of your feet, giving you better car feel and less fatigue.*

and you can't reach far enough to put it down all the way it will feel like you're dragging an anchor. So, modify the car to fit the driver. You want to be able to reach everything and feel everything when you're properly seated in the car.

Like the seat, the pedals are extremely important in conveying what the car is doing. The ball of your foot should be used when braking or operating the clutch. It is the strongest and most sensitive part of your foot. When not using the left foot (clutch foot) it should be near, but not on the clutch pedal. Some cars have a "dead-pedal," or solid resting point, but most don't. It is important to have a place to put your left foot to help brace you during hard cornering. If your car has no place to brace and rest your foot, you would do well to consider putting in a dead-pedal nearby at about the same height as the clutch pedal at rest. It's easy to do.

Maximum braking efficiency is *just before* a wheel locks up. Your foot must be taught, through practice and experience, what is the perfect pressure and what is too much. More about braking later, but like all the other controls it should be operated smoothly—squeezed on, not jumped on.

The same can be said for the throttle. Smooth. . .jump on the throttle of a 427 Cobra and see where you end up! For operating the throttle your heel should be firmly placed on the floor. This provides a pivot point to operate the throttle with the most control. It enables you to feed in the throttle in a smoother fashion. In a high-speed

*The proper hand position for shifting from first into second and third into fourth on a normal H-pattern gearbox. Treat the shift knob like an eggshell.*

drift, you are delicately balanced with throttle control. Just a bit too much can quickly send you off the road.

Before leaving the subject of pedals, it should be stressed that before you fire up your car be sure that your foot pedals and the bottom of your driving shoes (street shoes too) are dry and clean. It is distracting and dangerous if your shoes or pedals are oily or wet. If your shoe slips off the brake in the middle of the pack on the first lap, coming into the first turn at 100 + mph, you are in for a lesson you'd be better off without. The same thing applies in street traffic.

Let's give your feet a rest for now and put your hand (the right one, unless you have a right-hand drive car) to work. Shifting is one of the most basic things about driving a car. Shifting up to a higher gear is easy, but many even do that incorrectly. You should treat the gearshift lever like it was a fresh egg. By that we mean don't strangle or attack it, slamming it from gear to gear—you'll have egg all over your hand. Cup the palm of your hand on top of the gear lever and let your fingers extend down the lever shaft to provide guidance.

With a typical four- or five-speed-forward gearbox you'll have a basic H-pattern shift arrangement (with the fifth gear placed usually to the upper right, above reverse). To shift from first to second, place cupped palm of your hand on the lever, palm covering the knob, fingers down and use them to guide the lever back into second, gently. From second to third, just use the heel of the palm and the wrist, making sure to give it the necessary movement to the right at the neutral gate. Do it gently and smoothly; don't slam it. For the

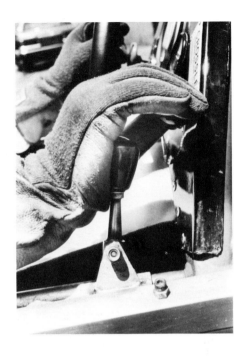

*And here's the correct method for shifting from second to third and fourth to fifth—use your wrist and gently guide the lever with the heel and palm of your hand. Smooth, clean shifts are much more important than fast shifts.*

shift from third to fourth, again use the fingers to guide it back; and for fourth to fifth use the heel to guide it up. You want to be firm and positive, but still gentle and smooth.

*I learned this method of shifting by accident. I was driving a BRM that was set up for Jackie Stewart. Jackie is considerably smaller than I am; his arms are short while mine are long. The only way I could get it in gear was to use a wrist action and the palm of my hand and my fingers because there was so little room in the cockpit. It worked so well that I kept doing it. Before that I, like most others, was trying to force it into gear making a fist around the lever. As it turned out, doing it right was not only easier but it really saved the gearboxes too.*

Speed in shifting is not really as important as a good clean shift. Not much is gained with a real fast shift, and it may cost you a transmission. In all of your operations be smooth and gentle on your car and it will be that much more reliable and fun to drive.

Proper down-shifting is a very important part in not only going fast but in driving your car to its full potential. Unless you learn to down-shift correctly you will never go really fast. Proper down-shifting is not easy. It requires much more coordination and concentration. This is the time to get everything working: both hands, both feet and, most difficult of all for some, the mind. Your left hand is steering, your right hand is shifting, your left foot is working the clutch and your right foot is not only braking but also rolling on and off the throttle to keep up the proper revs. That's not all—your ears are listening to the engine and gearbox sounds; your eyes are looking for your turn-in point for a corner, at your tach and maybe at the joker in your mirror. All of this is happening at the same time and to make things just a little worse, there's even more. Entering a corner you may also be passing someone or the guy behind might be putting a move on you or you may be trying to avoid some oil or a spin or trying to keep from spinning yourself. Maybe all at once. A lot going on. Fortunately, on the street it is a little easier than on the racetrack but the procedure to carry out a proper down-shift is the same.

The best way to learn your shifting and heel-and-toe is to practice it before you ever turn your car on, or roll it out of the garage. If you can't do it properly sitting still then you'll never get it right with the car moving.

*I find that the first problem most of my students have with down-shifting is a misconception. Many think that an important*

*It's not easy. You're steering with one hand, working the pedals with both feet and also paying attention to what's going on around you because...*

*...some joker may be putting a move on you. Here I'm following Bobby Unser, Jr., to evaluate his progress.*

*reason for down-shifting is to take advantage of the engine's brak-ing effect. That is a thought that has somehow survived from the days of skinny tires and rapidly fading drum brakes. Modern disc (and much more efficient drum) brakes or a good combination of both, have changed that. With modern brakes it's unnecessary and with modern engines it is a good way to break them.*

In racing, rev-limiters only work during acceleration, not dur-ing deceleration. That is, they cut the motor out at a fixed rev limit while under acceleration, but when a down-shift is made at too high a speed the engine has no choice but to over-rev if the clutch is let out too soon and proper braking hasn't been completed. If you over-rev, you may not break the engine right at that moment, but maybe a valve will be bent or stretched and before long it will show up and you'll need an engine rebuild, probably not even knowing why.

The goal when down-shifting is to change to a lower gear while maintaining maximum braking, without upsetting the car's weight transfer and balance. To do this there must be a perfect match be-tween engine, gearbox and rear wheel rpm (or front rpm on a front-wheel-drive), which requires your right foot to do "double-duty."

The technique required is called "heel-and-toe." Heel-and-toe is something of a misnomer, as most drivers use neither the heel nor the toe if the function is done properly. The term actually started in the fifties with Ferrari.

*Once, at Riverside, I was testing a 4.9-liter Ferrari and the pedals were set up for doing a true heel-and-toe. It was really a different arrangement, the clutch was on the left like it should be, but the throttle was in the middle and the brake was on the right. The reason was that the brakes in those days didn't stop very well, not like today. So it took a lot more muscle and foot pressure. With that car you could literally operate the gas with the heel while you pressed the brake with your toe or the ball of your foot. It seemed logical but the setup didn't last too long as it was just opposite to normal procedure on all of the production cars. I thought it was ok until one time I was entering turn nine at Riverside and forgot which was where for a second and I nearly crashed. I prefer the normal setup. This pedal arrangement has long since gone but the name has survived.*

As previously discussed, you should brake with the ball of your right foot, *not your toes,* this goes equally for proper heel-and-toe. Heel-and-toe is a function of down-shifting, so along with this, the procedure of "double-clutching" is used at the same time—the British refer to it as "double-declutching." Double-clutching can be done on the up-shift as well as on the down-shift but it is generally thought of as a down-shift function. To double-clutch by itself is a rather simple procedure. First you push in the clutch, move the shift lever out of gear and into the neutral gate, release the clutch about half-way, then depress it again instantly, continue your shift to the next desired gear and let the clutch out.

Now, to heel-and-toe. First the simple description of it alone, then we'll combine it with double-clutching and you'll have the complete down-shift. The simple function of the right foot in heel-and-toe is to, with the ball of the foot, brake for any given corner. At the same time the braking is being accomplished it is necessary to also rev the engine a predetermined amount with the right side of the right foot so that the clutching and shifting procedure can be completed at the same time. In simple terms, while braking with the ball of the right foot, the heel pivots to the right, still maintaining full braking pressure, and revs the throttle the proper amount, then pivots back to finish the braking or trail-braking procedure.

Now for the combined function, we'll move from fourth gear to third, a simple straight-forward down-shift, but the procedure is the same in any gear.

1) Start your braking procedure. Use the ball of your right foot, squeezing on the brake, increasing the pressure as necessary. Have your left foot in position to depress the clutch. (Don't push it in yet, just be ready.)

2) Move your hand to the shift lever, just use the palm of your hand cupped over the shift knob and your wrist. Continue your braking, add more pressure if necessary. Now push in the clutch while moving the shift lever from fourth to the neutral gate.

3) Continue braking, while letting out the clutch half-way (double-clutching). Now pivot your heel and roll the side of your right foot onto the throttle squeezing on the throttle, to rev up to a level just above where it will be in fourth gear ready to shift down to third.

4) Now push in the clutch again to complete the shift.

5) Pivot and roll your right heel back under the brake pedal completely after completing the shift from neutral to third, as you ease the clutch back out.

6) The clutch plates have taken hold and the revs weren't too high nor too low. Just nice and smooth. Continue braking and start to turn into the corner, gradually easing pressure off the brakes by a third of the way into the turn (trail-braking). Then you can smoothly bring in the throttle, accelerate to the apex and then out of the turn. Smooth. . .

As mentioned before it's best to practice with the car parked first. It seems like a lot of things to do in a very short time but you'll get so you can do the whole operation in a little more than one second. The revving of the throttle is very important during the procedure. The amount of revs somewhat depends on the individual car but the important thing is to match the speed of the engine to that of the gear you will be selecting. If the clutch is engaged with the rpm too low the rear wheels will lock up causing a skid. The best that can happen is that you will mess up the corner. The worst is you might damage your drivetrain, spin out or crash.

If you have too many rpm when you let the clutch out the car will be forced into acceleration, transferring weight to the rear with

**1**

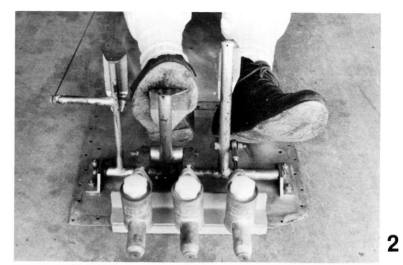

**2**

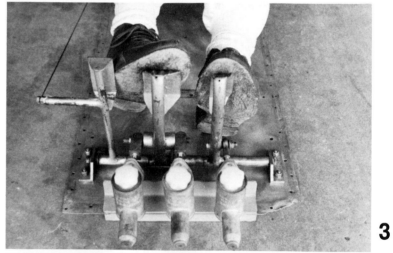

**3**

**4**

**5**

**6**

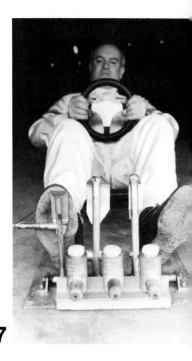

**7**

*Heel-and-toe/double-clutch sequence: 1—under acceleration with ball of right foot on throttle, left foot at rest. 2—right foot squeezes on brakes, slowing car and transferring weight forward onto front tires, left foot readies for double-clutch and shift (clutch not yet depressed). 3—left foot depresses clutch with ball of foot, right foot which is still braking pivots and rolls over on throttle to rev engine; shift is passing through neutral. 4—left foot releases clutch half way, right foot continues braking with throttle still on (car passes through neutral). 5—left foot fully depresses clutch with ball of foot, right foot continues braking with throttle at desired rpm, shift is completed to the lower gear. 6—left foot releases clutch smoothly as shift is completed and throttle is released as clutch plate starts to take hold, right foot pivots off throttle and starts trail-braking. 7—as trail-braking is completed the throttle is eased on.*

driving force (the engine is usually more powerful than the brakes) so you'll probably push right off the turn.

The real keys are that the engine rpm is matched with the rear wheel rpm when the gear change is made and the clutch is released smoothly. With some very responsive street cars you want to squeeze the throttle and hold it until the shift is complete. Then as you ease the clutch out ease off the throttle smoothly as the clutch is taking hold, for a smooth shift. Of course, to heel-and-toe properly the car must be correctly set up. That is to say, the throttle and the brake pedal must be arranged in a proximity to each other so when the brakes are fully compressed the brake pedal is still slightly higher and directly adjacent to the throttle.

One problem you can experience is brake fade, and a drop in pedal level. If your pedal level drops significantly during a heel-and-toe operation it is likely that you will inadvertently accelerate at the same time you are braking by catching your ankle on the side of the throttle pedal. This can be very detrimental to your braking effort! One solution is to learn to double-pump your brake pedal to bring it back up to pressure. But the best method is to, like all parts of your car, make sure your brakes are in good order and that you won't experience any unexpected problems.

To repeat, practice heel-and-toe with the car stopped and the motor off before you try it on the road. Get it down while you aren't moving in traffic. One more word of caution: Unless you have an electric fuel pump, chances are that while you sit in your car practicing the heel-and-toe and double-clutching you'll probably flood your engine and have trouble starting it after a half-hour of practice. Let the car sit for a few minutes so you can let the raw fuel evaporate. Then start the engine. If you have trouble starting your engine at that time, press the throttle to the floor and hold it there till the engine starts. If you have an electric fuel pump only, you won't have *that* problem because it only operates when the ignition (key) is on.

How about an automatic? Jim Hall's Chaparral had one, maybe your BMW or Ferrari has one too. Most people put their automatic transmission in drive and leave it there forever, except to back up. Use the second and the low ranges. That's what they are there for. For accelerating, use each of the gears, wind it out. Make the car work as it was intended to. As for down-shifting, you can't heel-and-toe, but your braking procedure is still the same. Use the ball of your foot. When you've braked sufficiently for a down-shift, move the lever to the gear you want, putting the weight transfer back to the rear. This could slightly help your braking, but remember to slow the car with the brakes, not the engine; and when you accelerate, just ease on the gas. With an automatic in top gear (drive) the engine back pressure (slowing force) is minimal, you'll only use this back pressure in the lower gears. For example, coming down a steep grade you should use your engine and it will help to reduce brake fade. In cornering, the lower gears of an automatic help the car's stability and responsiveness. Rather than using drive, use an appropriate lower gear along with the throttle and the car will steer around a turn much easier and safer.

*I don't recommend left-foot braking unless you learned it when you first learned to drive and have continued from that time on. You're using the throttle all of the time with your right foot and you develop a real delicate touch and feel with that foot which carries over to your braking, too. If, all of a sudden without a lot of previous practice, you start using your left foot on the brake you'll find that you haven't developed the needed sensitivity and you'll be locking up the brakes or not depressing them sufficiently to stop in time, especially in an emergency situation. In the Chaparrals it worked ok but you weren't dealing with power brakes; and the driver, Phil Hill, was a world champion too...*

*When I ran Indy you had left-foot braking so I had to practice for it especially. I practiced with an automatic and left-foot braking for two months before I ever got into the car. No matter what you decide on, the real key is to practice. You can practice and make it work but unless you have a real definite reason to brake with your left foot, I wouldn't bother. Use your practice time wisely...but* you *have to make the final decisions.*

*Smoothness is imperative; especially when controlling cars with high horse-power-to-weight ratios such as this Cobra Daytona Coupe. You really had to be aggressively smooth.*

As you've figured out by now, down-shifts are not easy to master and when you do learn to get them right, they need constant practice and attention. The best thing about shifting is that it can be practiced every day in your normal driving.

To go really quickly you have to get all the parts to work together. Practice them. Give them your time and your attention. Feeling more comfortable with your 500-horsepower Superbird? Great . . .Now let's get to know your car even better!

# CHAPTER FIVE

# Getting To Know Your Car

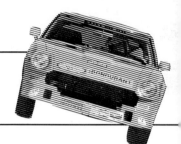

Your car's particular balance is monitored by the tires, steering and chassis. Your seating and steering-wheel position are so important because these are your sensor probes telling you just what the car is doing at all times. These sensor probes enable you to make use of the entire one-hundred percent of the theoretical traction limit available. To make full use of all your sensors, you must have faith that your car is giving you correct input. This means that your car must be properly maintained and prepared. The value of proper maintenance and preparation really pays off in fewer problems, more enjoyable driving and a substantial saving of money on costly repairs that will be minimal if caught early enough.

*When racing the BRM Formula One car, I was confronted with the problem of maintenance. At the Nürburgring I was having a great battle going with the factory Ferraris of Lorenzo Bandini, Ludovico Scarfiotti and Mike Parkes, when a camshaft broke. I missed the next race at the Dutch Grand Prix because the engine was being rebuilt and it didn't get back in time (two engines would have been a luxury for the under-financed team).*

*The car arrived at Monza "ready to race." I found that the only thing that had been touched on the car was to put the engine back in. At Nürburgring it had rained during the whole race. When I looked over the car I could see rust spots still all over it.*

*Airborne at the Nürburgring shortly before the broken camshaft put me out of the race while running fourth battling the factory Ferraris.*

*I couldn't believe it. All they did was take the engine out, park it and when the engine came back, they just put it back in. They hadn't touched the car other than that. So, I walked around the car, found a few nuts and bolts that were a half-turn loose, a full-turn loose and some that weren't even there. I was disgusted. I grabbed a handful of wrenches and went over the whole car. I re-set the chassis and tightened all the nuts and bolts. It didn't go well that day. I really didn't trust the car, as no one had maintained it. During the race I could never really get going up to full potential. I think I ran about ninth. That was my last ride with the team. After the race I quit, seeing that it wasn't going to get any better.*

Proper preparation of your car is vital, be it a racing car or a street car. In racing, a driver is certainly not going to win unless he finishes. A well-maintained car is a must. The costs of having a car maintained and prepared are high so, assuming you have a certain amount of mechanical competency, do as much of the maintenance and preparation as you can. This goes for both the street or the race-track. The better that you know your car the better driver you will be. If you know nothing of mechanics try to find time to take a class at your local college or high school—you are investing in yourself.

Before you attempt to work on your car, make sure you have a complete set of the necessary tools. In addition to the standard tools make sure you have the specialized ones that your particular car may require. Nothing is more discouraging than wasting an hour to do something that, with the proper tool, could have been done in a minute. Of great importance is to buy good-quality tools. A cheap wrench or socket will spread, or round. It can do expensive damage to the part you are trying to fix.

While you are becoming a first-rate mechanic, with meticulous work habits and good tools, it is also important to have a good place in which to work. Nothing, and I mean nothing, can make working on your car more unpleasant than a cramped, cold, dirty and poorly lit work area. Try to have a place that has enough room, that is clean (like your car should be) and has enough light and is well heated to make what you are doing both easy and pleasurable. Preparing a race car will take lots of hours; make sure your investment is secure in a properly laid out, well lit, clean and warm work area. Those preparation hours will be much more pleasant and more productive.

When preparing a race car (not a bad idea for maintaining a street car either), use a check list. Actually, it will take three separate ones.

1) A specific list of work to do on the car.
   a. routine checks and maintenance
   b. repairs to be done
   c. potential trouble spots to be checked
2) A standard list of each step in the preparation process.
3) A list of each item that you will be taking with you to the races.

Without check lists, trying to prepare a race car and getting it to the track with everything you need can be a chaotic undertaking.

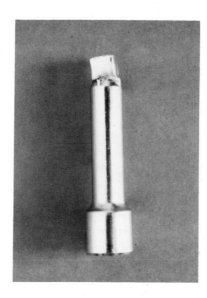

*Good-quality tools; always! Imagine trying to get an accurate torque reading using this socket extension.*

*Meticulous preparation pays off not only in a good-looking race car but one that will be reliable—especially important on a high-stress course like Monza. This Ferrari Dino was fantastically prepared—a car you could really feel confident with at the limit.*

Race car or street car, small problems left unattended have a way of producing major consequences. A leaking fuel line, little hang-ups in the throttle linkage, decreasing brake fluid reservoir—all these things and many more can lead to expensive confrontations of one kind or another. If you work a full-time job and do all of your own car preparation and maintenance then your time will be at a premium. Work on a priority basis. First, take care of everything that could adversely affect your car's *safety*. Then concentrate on those things that will affect your car's *reliability*. The last concern to you should be with modifications for *performance*.

If you are preparing for racing, what wins is meticulous and methodical preparation to ensure that your car functions properly. There is no black magic involved. A large distinction should be made between race car preparation and race car development: The major expenditure in race preparation is time. The major expenditure in race car development is money. Of course, time is money but in development it takes a lot of time in addition to a great deal of money.

*If you are interested in race car preparation then I recommend a book that was written by Carroll Smith, Shelby's crew chief for the factory Cobras and GT 40's. It is titled* Prepare to Win, *and it is excellent. Smith's book outlines step by step what should be done, how it should be done and what tools are necessary to properly prepare a racing car. Required reading!*

*Performance modifications and having the "trickest" car at the circuit are neat, but they are also very expensive. Also, if you are continually trying new trick parts there is a good chance that* *you won't know how your car should be actually running or handling and you won't know where to pinpoint your troubles because of confused or mixed input coming back to you. What you should be primarily concerned with, is learning how to drive your car the best that you can. If you are on a tight budget, use your money to become a first-class driver. Keep your car clean and well maintained; but if it comes to a choice of $75 for a trick part or $75 for a day of practice, spend the money practicing. In a year or two that car will probably be sold and you'll have a faster, tricker and better one, but your skill as a driver will always be with you. Invest in yourself. . .it always stays with you.*

It is important to have a car that is properly maintained so that it can be depended on to react in the same fashion each time it is called on to do so. By doing your own maintenance and preparation, and doing it thoroughly, you know your car better and can trust it more completely.

Along with good maintenance goes cleanliness. Keep the car clean—not simply the outside, but keep it clean in the engine compartment and underneath, too. Don't let dirt build up. If it does, you won't be able to spot a loose nut or bolt, or an oil leak. That oil leak

*A well-lighted, well-equipped and clean place to work on your car is essential.*

may be from the pan, or maybe a main-bearing, or even the oil filter gasket or sump plug that's about to fall out and dump all your oil.

To know your car takes a lot of time learning and checking everything but it pays off in a mind at ease, that can concentrate on driving, not on worrying what's going to fall off next, or if the brakes are going to work at the next turn. If you know your car and can trust it and its preparation, you'll be miles ahead of the competition both on the street or on the track. Besides, you don't want to keep your 500-horsepower brute parked on the street, do you?

# CHAPTER SIX
## Getting To Know Yourself

**M**aking your car perform up to its full potential takes a total effort. The delicate balance between braking, cornering and acceleration is a balance of self.

This is a balance that, as you learn and practice it, permits you to recognize and maintain one-hundred-percent car control at all times. Every bit of practice, on the street or the racetrack, helps to facilitate a full and complete blending of functions, ultimately arriving at a precise control of the car. The old adage, "Practice makes perfect" is, when it comes to driving, correct. Practice builds smoothness and consistency but they are governed by a very important element that enables it to all happen: concentration.

While driving on the street, there are many distractions that constantly bombard your concentration. At normal speeds these lapses are into the never-never land of radio, billboards, neat-looking cars, attractive pedestrians and just about any other distraction that you can think of. On the street, usually all that happens is that you slow down to take it all in. The possibility of a slight fender-bender is an everpresent danger if you really become occupied with something that doesn't fit in with your driving. That's on the street. . .It's a lot different on the racetrack.

In racing, concentration is an absolute must. There is no other way if you are to be successful and at the same time safe. A slight lapse in concentration for just a moment, even a *fraction of a second,*

*Concentrate and plan your race. . . even before the race begins it's especially important no matter where you are on the grid.*

can cause you to miss a shift or an apex, spin, blow an engine or crash. If you lose concentration all of this can happen, and more.

As important as concentration is, it is no guarantee that you will go fast. Your concentration may be flawless but you may be doing the same thing wrong in precisely the same way time after time. Practice building concentration. Then concentrate on the proper way to drive and being consistently smooth—your ultimate goal. Concentration + Technique + Consistency = Smoothness.

Smoothness takes a lot of self-discipline. But, smooth is fast, and smooth is safe. Smoothness is more than just an aspect of technique, it is virtually a state of mind. Cars respond positively to firm, consistent and gentle treatment. Smoothness is not doing just one thing smooth, but everything. It is the way you handle the steering wheel, the relaxed but alert way you sit, the way you squeeze on or ease off the brakes and throttle. It is the precise way you change gears and the sensitivity you have to everything your car is doing under you. Anyone can do it but some do it better. Some have more sensitivity and feel and are naturally smoother. But lots of practice and good instruction can only make you better. When driving slowly it is not as noticeable but when driving a high performance car fast, smoothness really makes a difference in how fast you go.

The most difficult factor in the equation is consistency. All that you do in a car is interrelated. If you are inconsistent or erratic in just one aspect of your driving it negatively affects all the rest and consequently smoothness is lost. Smoothness is the sum total of everything that you do in a car. It is derived from sensitivity, prolonged by consistency and made possible by unrelenting concentration and car feel! If you want to race, smoothness is helpful. . .if you want to win, it's *essential.*

*I remember when Dave MacDonald and I were racing against each other in Corvettes. Dave was fast, one of the fastest drivers around. But he would be slipping and sliding all over the track, spending about as much time sideways as he did going in a straight line. Part of it was his car but most of it was his style. Dave and I both went about the same speed most of the time. If Dave would have refined and smoothed out his style I know that he would have been able to go even that much faster. He was a great natural talent.*

*Natural talent is having a certain sense and feel about the control of the car. An up-and-coming driver who exhibits a lot of this but not in the sideways sense of MacDonald, Ronnie Peterson or Gilles Villeneuve is Michele Alboreto. It's having the control over your own emotions and the self discipline to drive with complete car feel. This is an extremely disciplined sport and it's really hard not to let yourself slip into the area of driving with a lot of oversteer which is great fun but usually not as fast as if one were clean and smooth. It's really fun to pitch a car sideways and it*

*If you want to win, smoothness is essential. And winning can be a lot of fun.*

*really looks neat but it's just not as fast. Early on those drivers learned how to control their cars in adverse conditions, when the cars didn't work well and so on. But later in their careers they became smoother and more precise driving at the absolute limit; perhaps just a fraction past the normal limit because of their great control. As you go faster and faster and as the cars become better, the margin of control becomes much finer. That's where the self discipline comes in. You must have the delicate feel for keeping the car in balance. The bottom line is that even natural talent still has to be trained. You still have to learn, to perfect and refine.*

Just because you see a stab-n-steer driver going the same speed or faster than a smoother driver it doesn't mean that the two styles are equally effective. All it means is that the stab-n-steer driver is driving well below his potential and could be going even faster. If speed and safety aren't reason enough, driving smooth is also much more reliable.

When you look at the records of some of the world's best drivers you will notice that they had an exceptionally high finishing rate. Drivers like Juan Manuel Fangio, Jackie Stewart, Jim Clark, Niki Lauda and Carlos Reutemann were not just fast but their finish records were fantastic. Fangio competed in fifty-one Grand Prix races

*Taken at Sebring in 1964, here I am with Carroll Shelby and the great Jimmy Clark. Jimmy won two world championships, Indy and more than a third of his Formula One races—not just finished, but won them. He was smoothness and consistency personified as well as the "real master" of trailbraking.*

but he won twenty-four of them, five World Championships and averaged 5.44 world championship points per race in which he competed. That's not too bad when you consider that all you get for a win is nine points. Stewart won twenty-seven out of ninety-nine races, three World Championships and averaged 3.64 points per race. Clark won twenty-five out of seventy-two races, two World Championships and averaged 3.81 points per race. Lauda and Reutemann also show that this consistency is a characteristic of great competitors. Reutemann has the all-time record for finishing consecutive Grand Prix in the points: fifteen in a row. This spanned two seasons of racing, 1980 and '81. Fangio is second with fourteen straight in three seasons, 1953, '54, '55. Clark reached twelve in a row and Lauda eleven without a miss. Like they say you can't win if you don't finish.

A smooth, fluid driver who effortlessly blends one function into the next is easy on his car, saving it unnecessary stress and wear. The brakes, engine, transmission, suspension—the entire car—have a better chance of lasting if you are smooth. That is just as important for driving on the street. Make your car last.

*To develop good concentration, proper technique and the all-important smoothness requires practice, practice, practice. Just like when you took piano lessons as a kid. Practice whenever you drive. If you are a racer, use the time you drive on the street as practice. I don't mean blasting around town at high speeds, but do take the time when you drive to concentrate on what you need to improve. It is easy to improve your braking and down-shifting, double-clutch and heel-and-toe while driving on the street. It is also a good place to practice cornering—not by going excessively fast but just by doing it properly, looking ahead for the proper apex and exit.*

*I was to do a hill climb in Germany that was one of the World Manufacturers events. I'd never run a hill climb before and this road was a normal highway that would be blocked off for the hill climb on race day only. I was to drive the Cobra, but there was no way I could before the event. I wanted to get to know the road so I took the Volkswagen that I had and each morning about 5 a.m. I drove up and down the hill. It was a real rough climb, lots of sharp bends and it ran for about eight miles. What I did, even though I was driving a little VW, was to think and to react and to put in my mind what the Cobra would be like at all the different parts of the course—where it would understeer, where it would oversteer, where it would be in a four-wheel drift. I was amazed how much I learned flogging that little VW up that hill. It was a challenge of mind, not of speed.*

Smoothness is the work of methodically blending functions. In the beginning it is infinitely more important to be smooth than to be fast. Fast comes later. Concentrate on learning to drive smoothly and properly before concerning yourself with going fast. When you first

*Always focus your eyes ahead, where you want to go. Input from your eyes is your number one source of information.*

try to make all the functions blend together you'll probably feel like a cow on ice. Don't be discouraged and don't worry about speed or how long it takes you to develop the skill. You must learn how to go smooth slowly before you will ever go smooth quickly. It takes a lot of time and it is difficult to achieve. That's probably the reason very few drivers ever really accomplish it.

A major part in achieving this smoothness is your *hand/eye co-ordination.* Certainly you steer the car with your hands and arms but your eyes tell you what to do. Your eyes actually lead your physical movement. Your hands act upon the information that your eyes feed them. Focus your eyes where you want to go not where you are, or where you *don't* want to go. Look ahead; don't drive off the nose of the car. Focus all the time on what's happening ahead so you have plenty of time to make the necessary corrections to the car if there is an emergency. If there is a turn coming up, you have the proper time to read how to enter it.

Good hand/eye coordination is a skill that is developed through practice. The more you can practice it, the better it will become. There are exercises that you can do with your eyes to improve them and what they tell you. There are also many activities, sports and games that will, while affording you a good time, improve your co-ordination and, at the same time, your physical condition. For the eye exercises, contact your eye doctor for recommendations to improve your vision and the strength of your eyes. There are exercises that will increase your peripheral vision and others to improve your eye muscles. Keep them strong, they are your number one source of information.

As for your coordination, sports such as handball, racket ball, tennis, ping pong and the like do help improve coordination and reaction time. All of them enhance driving skills. They all involve the basic physical requirements for driving and racing: endurance, balance, fast reflexes and good hand/eye and foot/eye coordination. It is just as necessary to have these assets available to you driving on the street, especially if you fancy driving the back roads hard and fast.

On the racing circuit, if you are to be any good at all you must be in good shape. Driving a racing car is more mentally and physically demanding than those not involved could ever imagine. Coping with g forces in cornering, working the steering or the brakes, and functioning in extreme heat take strength and endurance. The heat generated by a race car amplifies the exertion required. And all the physical exertion is nothing compared to the mental exertion. The real sapper of strength and the primary reason for being in prime shape is the very intense and unyielding concentration you must maintain. A driver who is not fit will be worn down by the mental exertion. This produces exaggerated fatigue and that makes your concentration and coordination suffer even more. The best you can hope for is a poor performance, not to mention the increased possibility of an accident. The better your physical condition is, the better you will do at driving. Likewise, the better you get at other sports the better you will do in a car. You want to develop a good mental and physical condition, increase your coordination and concentration, prolong your endurance and improve your reaction speed.

*The stress of concentration and strain of physical exertion can take a tremendous toll on a racing driver's body. Long grueling races and the car's heat (especially in a closed vehicle such as the Ford GT 40 or the current Groupe C cars) all accentuate the need to be in good physical condition. This car with its 540 horsepower really could wear you down fast if you weren't in top shape.*

In racing you must know where your physical and mental limitations are. Part of this can be discovered through other sports and competitive activities such as skiing, bicycling and jogging. In making his comeback to racing, Niki Lauda spent the better part of six months improving his physical condition. He did miles of jogging and skiing in addition to other exercises and regular work-outs. Running, especially in competition, is like car racing. At the start, you push to go quickly for the first third of the race, settle into a groove for the second third then push for a strong finish, pacing yourself the whole way to make sure you do finish. Sports and working out teach you self-discipline and how to pace yourself. It all helps you to learn your limitations.

If you are in good physical condition you can drive long and hard and not tire. On the other hand, if you are overweight and not very physically active, then you'll tire quickly. It gets very hot in a race and during a long race it is easy to lose eight or ten pounds just in fluids. This is demanding and exhausting. If you aren't in good condition for those kinds of demands on your body then you won't hold up. In a recent race at Daytona, one team had a young driver in good condition, while the other two on the team were in less-than-prime shape. The young driver ended up doing double-duty in driving stints and finally the drivers who were in poor condition quit and turned their drive over to another driver who was in good shape. It was an expensive waste.

*I find rowing a scull is excellent for physical conditioning.*

If you want to race but are not in good physical condition, you are wasting both your time and money. Don't impose unnecessary risks and limitations on yourself. Get in shape. It's work but it can be fun too. There are many games that increase your reaction speed and hand/eye coordination; not just physical sports like tennis, skiing and handball. A very good and popular alternative is the current new video games. They are excellent for the mind. They are great for anticipating what is coming up and for improving your reaction speed.

Mental conditioning is unquestionably the most important conditioning that you can do. Keep sharp, fast and alert by keeping your mind active. When you race, you have to use strategy. Many leisure games help to promote this. Good examples are chess and backgammon. These kinds of games help you to make decisions, and quickly. One wrong decision in a race car can quickly make you lose, oftentimes in a big way. A delayed decision is just as bad. Do all that you can to improve your total conditioning.

Remember that your car is but a small part of driving. You are what makes the car last or breaks it, the one who maintains it properly or lets it go. You are the one who learns to combine all the driving aspects into a smooth and flowing motion or is herky-jerky. You are the only one responsible for your ultimate performance. Build on yourself. Improve all that you do, physically and mentally. The more you know and the better condition you are in, the better you will

*Video games are a good way to improve your mental as well as hand/eye coordination.*

become at everything. Add that to driving practice and who knows, you could become great.

Since you are your best judge and worst critic, do it for yourself. Learn how to control yourself and to be in control of yourself. Racing is a total commitment if you are to be successful. On the street you can perhaps be a good driver even if you are a little out of shape and your reactions are a bit slow but on the track it can kill you, or someone else.

Enough lecture. We are about ready to take your 500-horsepower monster out of the garage and see what it feels like to combine all your braking and shifting practice on the road. Let's try to get you into the corners—better yet, out of them—safely and quickly.

# CHAPTER SEVEN
# *Getting Behind The Wheel*

*It doesn't matter what kind of car you have; if you get to know it and learn to drive it properly, it can be a great source of enjoyment. There seems to be an increasing number of engine/drive-train configurations on the road today—from the old tried-and-true front engine/rear-wheel drive, to front engine/front drive, rear engine/rear drive, mid-engine/rear drive and four-wheel drive. Each performs somewhat differently and has its own handling characteristics. For that matter, each individual car differs from another of the same model. What it takes is getting used to a particular car through actual driving time and practice. What I can give you are the basics of why cars act in a particular fashion in a given circumstance—theory backed up by practice, testing and lots of experience.*

The key to successful high performance driving, on the street or on the racetrack, is one easy, simple thing: *maximizing traction!* Traction is the cohesive factor between the tires and the road surface. The primary goal of a driver should be to control his car to consistently take advantage of every bit of traction that is theoretically available. The basic functions of braking, shifting, cornering and accelerating have one prime objective: maximizing traction.

In racing, the closer a driver gets to complete utilization of the theoretical limit of traction, the faster he will go.

*During the functions of braking, cornering and acceleration each car has its theoretical limit of traction. This limit is determined by the tires, suspension, chassis, weight and balance of the car and the abrasive level of the road surface. Notice I first mentioned tires. The other components of this limit, each in its own way, affect the tires to either add or subtract traction.*

Maximum traction is achieved by controlling weight transfer which is, in essence, getting the shifting and moving mass of the car over the desired wheels to push those tires into maximum contact with the road.

The area of tire in contact with the surface of the road is referred to as the "tire patch." The maximum traction that you can possibly have is limited or enhanced directly by the total tire patch area. It is possible to have the greatest area of traction where it's not wanted, causing all sorts of problems in cornering and braking, not to mention acceleration.

When a car is sitting motionless, the largest tire patch areas are determined by the physical weight balance of the car. In a conventional car (front engine/transmission and rear drive) the weight is normally distributed near the ratio of fifty to fifty-six percent front and fifty to forty-four percent at the rear. This will usually give a slightly larger tire patch at the front than at the rear due to the slightly heavier front end. With a rear engine/rear drive the weight ratio usually runs forty-four to fifty percent at the front and fifty-six to fifty percent at the rear, just reversing the weight bias to the rear tire patch. With front engine/front drive vehicles the weight distribution is much more forward-biased with a ratio of approximately sixty percent front to forty percent rear, thus making the front tire patches the largest. The mid-engined car will run a near-neutral weight distribution as well as tire patch.

Now, when you put this in motion you have added the resistance to movement of the basic weight of the car. This weight shift moves to the rear as a car accelerates, adding some area to the rear tire patch. As the car brakes, that force shifts to the front, adding area to the front tire patch. This resistance and weight movement is called weight transfer.

Weight transfer not only moves forward and backward but also laterally. In cornering, when the car is in the first third of the turn and you are maintaining a trail-brake, the weight transfer is not only coming forward but is also directed away from the corner you are turning into. When turning right, the transfer of weight will be to the left front corner, increasing the tire patch on the left front wheel. Turning to the left, the transfer goes to the right front.

The balance during the transition between braking and accelerating is a very delicate one because as you accelerate you are transferring the weight again to the rear. During acceleration in a turn to the right the weight and increased tire patch area move to the left rear; and conversely, to the right rear in a left-hand turn. This transfer of weight amplifies the need for smoothness. Any abrupt movement in weight transfer, especially at the time of transition between braking and acceleration—that is, too much too fast of either braking, lack of braking, acceleration or lack of acceleration—will drastically alter your weight balance and, consequently, your tire patch may send you for a ride through the bushes.

Weight is continually transferred as a car moves through acceleration, braking and cornering. Your goal is to make the weight transfer harmonize with the needs of the suspension and tires to achieve optimum traction. With a racing car you want to constantly blend your braking into cornering, your cornering into acceleration and your acceleration into braking, keeping in mind all the time that you want to be at, but not past, the limit of maximum traction.

*If you are not accomplishing these transitions in one fluid motion, then you might be one of those that I refer to as the "stab-n-steer" group. Most highway drivers fall into this category if they are trying to drive fast. Likewise, the vast majority of racing drivers (that includes many top national competitors) don't put the whole package together either; and a good percentage of them are also of the stab-n-steer variety. Their theory is simply to go as fast as the car can go, brake as hard and late as possible, then drive around any given corner as fast as they can and get as much power on as fast as they are able. Those guys are fun to watch and fun to photograph because their cars are always out of shape and you can expect them to run off a turn at least once during a race. But, that's not truly fast in terms of lap times and it's awfully hard on equipment.*

*A typical stab-n-steer driver charges into a turn, executes a late, banzai braking attempt, does a herky-jerky down-shift and jumps off the brakes (transferring the weight to the rear thereby reducing the traction available for steering). He next pounces on the throttle (putting even more weight transfer to the rear, making steering even more tricky) then has to come off the throttle because the car starts to either oversteer or understeer too much (coming off the throttle transfers the weight again to the front so the steering comes back). Then he is on and off the throttle and correcting the steering all the way around the corner. This is not fast, nor is it safe.*

In the next chapter we'll detail an actual cornering sequence. The main point now is to get you to realize the importance of weight transfer because it is weight transfer that determines the amount of traction you will have available. Once you get weight transfer working for you, you must keep it working. This is accomplished by very precise, almost delicate, use of the car's controls.

**REAR**

*John Blakemore and I worked out a way to show you the actual effects of weight transfer on the tire patch of a car. This may vary slightly with the size and kind of tire as well as the car, but in concept it can be used for a base of reference. These examples are from a Formula Ford; the rear tires are larger than the front tires. Here is the car at rest.*

 **FRONT**

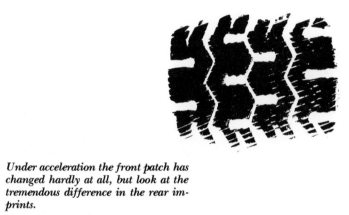 

**REAR**

*Under acceleration the front patch has changed hardly at all, but look at the tremendous difference in the rear imprints.*

**FRONT**

**REAR**

*And when you hit the binders the car's weight shifts dramatically toward the front.*

**FRONT**

**REAR**

*Here are our tire patches during a right hand corner. Lateral weight transfer in a corner is very pronounced, and evident in this example. Note that even within the left front tire patch itself, the outside (left) edge is being forced into the pavement moreso than the inside edge of the tread.*

As you get to know your particular car you will learn its particular balance. Learning how to drive your car the best that you can is one of your primary goals—the foremost reason you bought this book. To really get to know your car means lots of time behind the wheel finding out about the limits of the car and you. If your car is used primarily on the street, then it may be difficult as well as dangerous to find those limits. Discover those limits where you, your car or anyone else will not be hurt. Look for competitive events such as slaloms, autocrosses, rallys and racing schools that will allow you to find the limits of your car and yourself, safely.

The primary goal of a driver is control and that means maximum traction!

# CHAPTER EIGHT

# Getting To Know The Road

**N**ow that you are seated properly, holding your steering wheel correctly, have your pedals adjusted just right, have gotten yourself in good physical and mental condition, and understand the importance of maximizing traction, let's move on down the road. Remember the basics: Concentrate, be smooth and be consistent. If you can put all of this together then you have already become a better driver than when you picked up this book.

Welcome, now, to the most difficult corner in the world! That reference could apply to any turn in the world as viewed by any driver. Every driver has his own kind of problem turns. Do you have a particular kind of turn in which you feel clumsy and slow? Do you know how to read a turn properly? How about doing it right after you've read it?

*What is a turn anyway? Simply, it's an entrance or an exit to a straight-away. I'm going to tell you how to do it the safest, most stable and fastest way possible. First of all, if you have a street car, with regular street tires, before you even think about driving hard, make sure you have sufficient pressure. At my school all the cars are run with at least thirty-four pounds of pressure in each tire. Use this as a starting guide. If you don't have enough air in the tires you can pull a tire right off the rim during hard cornering, which can cause a nasty accident. More about tires later, but make sure you have enough air, and by that I mean about ten pounds more than the recommended street pressures or the side-wall will compress and it can come off the rim.*

Any given corner can be broken up into three segments: entry, apex area and exit. The entry to a turn is the most important part. Your entry dictates all that will follow—where, how fast and how stable you exit. Also it is the primary factor in how fast you go on the following straight-away. The entry of the turn is where you combine braking and the double-clutch, heel-and-toe and down-shift (that you've been so diligently working on) into one fluid movement.

Before we get into lines of a turn, good ones and bad ones, let's concentrate on how to do the steps of a corner properly:

*I am in a racing car and heading down the straight-away at 140 mph, ahead is a simple ninety-degree right-hand turn that can be completed at 90 mph. As I approach the turn my eyes are feeding me input about the road, turn and traffic while the input I am receiving from the car is telling me exactly what it is doing.*

*As I approach the turn from the left edge of the available road (about one foot from my left wheel to the road edge) I am under full acceleration. I sight my braking point (shut-off point). I ease off the gas (don't jerk off the gas or you pitch the car's weight forward rather than transferring it forward smoothly) and firmly but gently squeeze the brakes on with the ball of my foot. The weight is being smoothly transferred to the front wheels, expanding the front tire patches. I apply maximum brake but I balance my pressure so that the wheels don't lock up. I use the brakes (not the engine) to slow the car. Now, before I enter the corner, it is necessary to complete the down-shift. For this turn, I have gone down from fourth to third.*

*Entering a late apex area. The car is stable but in a four-wheel drift under full acceleration. All four tire patches are working at the limit—my line and my exit point are committed.*

*Because of the heavy braking, maximum traction is on the front wheels, assuming that you haven't locked up the brakes. Remember to keep looking where you want to be going.*

*With the car going its slowest I reach my turn-in point, continue major braking and turn into the corner. This is accomplished by giving a slightly exaggerated steering movement into the turn. This short but abrupt turn of the steering wheel transfers the forward weight laterally and "sets" the chassis—further squeezing down on the springs and suspension, compressing the shock absorbers and increasing the tire patch. The left front (outside) wheel now carries the majority of the adhesion for steering and cornering. I've used maximum braking while entering the turn but as I turn into the first third of the corner I begin to trail-brake. This keeps the chassis set while I aim for the apex area and increases the tire patch for cornering.*

*When setting up for a corner get your down-shift completed just prior to turning in. That is, start your braking and, while braking, execute your heel-and-toe down-shift from fourth to third to second (or you can down-shift directly from fourth to second but only after you've slowed to a second-gear speed). If you down-shift too soon you may well over-rev the engine and bend a valve. As soon as you complete the down-shift, the clutch pedal is released smoothly and the right heel pivots back below the brake pedal which allows you to start easing pressure off the brake pedal ever so smoothly and gradually, finishing the release about the first third of the entry into the corner, then picking up throttle heading for the apex and the exit onto the straight-away.*

*As the car tracks into the corner, heading for the apex area, my right foot, slowly and precisely with a high rate of feeling and sensitivity, starts to ease its way off the brake. All I'm doing by this time is dragging the brake pucks on the disc. The dragging puck keeps the chassis set. I am not using this last stage of trail-braking to slow down; that was done as I was first entering the corner. The way you can tell when you've reached the limit of trail-braking is when the back end of the car starts to get a little bit light and begins to slide out. When it reaches that point, I smoothly come all the way off the brake and start to squeeze the throttle on, transferring the weight smoothly to the rear tires. I do this as two separate motions. Don't slide your foot from the brake to the throttle, move it positively.*

*The first third of the corner is nearing completion as the throttle is being eased in and I am looking toward the apex area. The balance of throttle is very important at this point. I ease in as much throttle as the rear wheels will take. If the rear wheels start to lose traction, I ease off the throttle a bit to recover adhesion. I don't keep my foot all the way in it. That won't work properly because the tires will heat up and the traction goes away sooner.*

*Passing through the second third of the corner, the apex area, the car is now in the most stable condition it will be in, until after the exit onto the straight-away. The car is now under throttle control and all four tire patches are working for me. The steering is set for the exit and I am starting to look at the exit point. This second third of the corner is a very important transitional stage.*

*My line through the turn has been set and I am committed. Too much gas and too much weight will transfer and the traction will be upset. This will cause too much weight to come off the front tires causing me to lose front tire adhesion and put the car into an understeer condition. The weight transfer is being gradually moved to the rear of the car during acceleration. I ease onto the gas to maintain the forward stability and the suspension set. As I feed in more throttle I am increasing the rear tire patches while at the same time adjusting the transfer of weight from the outside front to the outside rear of the car. My acceleration is picked up more now and increases to full throttle heading for the exit of the turn. Continually, I am focusing my eyes, not where I am, but where I want to go.*

To backtrack just a bit, exactly what is the *apex area* we keep referring to? Most books just call it "apex" or "clipping point." This is a little bit of a misrepresentation. True, there is a geometric apex of a turn that's right in the middle of the turn. And the clipping point is where your inside front wheel is physically closest to the inside edge of the corner. Forget the apex, forget the clipping point! What you want to learn about is the driving apex area. We say apex *area* because its length varies. Every freeway off-ramp, mountain curve,

*Parking lot autocross or gymkhana events can teach you a lot about controlling your car. Here I'm following a student through a similar setup at my old Orange County facility, in our original Datsun school cars.*

racetrack corner or highway turn has an apex area. Some even have two. But every turn has at least one.

The variable factor in an apex area is the speed at which you hit the apex area combined with the length (or radius) of the curve. If, for example, you have a very slow corner, say on the street, you might have a very short apex area. But on a very high-speed turn on a race course the apex area might be four or five car lengths. It really depends on the speed potential of the given turn. Slow or fast, street or track, you want to hit the apex area properly to get maximum traction, stability and acceleration out of the turn. The apex area is the part of the turn when your car is in the most stable condition. A longer apex area is necessary when driving or racing in the rain. Let's get back to the 90-mph right-hand turn.

*I am now feeding in full throttle and the centrifugal force is pushing my car to the outside edge of the turn. I have full traction for acceleration and I'm heading toward my chosen exit point. The apex area that I chose was about two thirds of the way around the turn. My turn-in point to the corner was deeper and later than if I would have had a mid-point apex area. By having a relatively late apex area, I have ensured that when I am under full throttle, the forces acting on the car will not push it too far to the outside, and off the road, at the exit. The car is heading pretty much in a straight line as I approach and then leave the apex area.*

*This last third of the corner, the exit, is the easiest part if I did everything preceding right; if I didn't, it will become the most difficult. Remember, you always want to exit long and wide in order to dissipate the unsettling forces which pick up momentum when the speed increases. I have chosen a long and wide exit using all of the road possible. I will be easing out the correction of my steering, smoothly, as I aim in a straight line for the exit point. Under full throttle, my car is on the border of maximum traction and I am now in a slight drift—almost to the exit point. As I hit my exit point, I am already looking down the straight-away for the next turn.*

If you're practicing this turn and your turn-in point was correct, you hit the proper apex area for your speed and the car, then you should still be on the correct line to be able to use the maximum road available at the exit. If you did everything right you were definitely faster than you were before you began using these techniques. You have left your old driving habits behind.

In racing, remember that the earlier you can ease into full throttle in a corner, the faster you will enter the straight-away. The faster you enter the straight-away the sooner you reach maximum speed. The sooner you reach maximum speed the faster you get to the next corner. If you can reach full speed thirty yards earlier, you can carry that speed for the entire distance of the straight-away. On one turn you may gain two or three tenths of a second. Add that little bit plus nine or ten turns and, surprise, you've knocked a couple of seconds

*A corner composite. The numbers on the photo indicate the following actions: 1—under full braking. 2—start heel-and-toe down shift. 3—complete down-shift. 4—start trail-braking. 5—complete trail-braking. 6—begin acceleration. 7—under full acceleration. 8—exit point. 9-10—this is the apex area. To put all of this in perspective, this section can be driven in approximately six to seven seconds.*

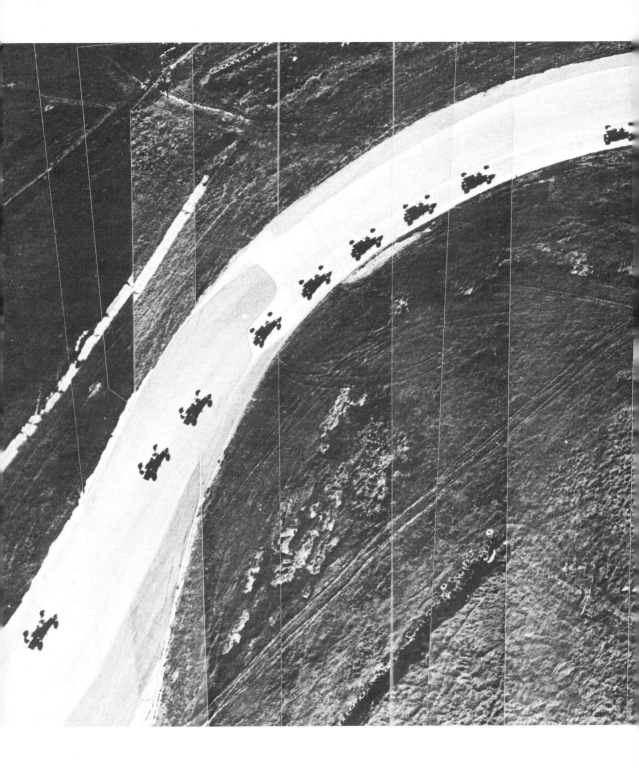

*The proper entry and exit of a typical 90-degree turn. Note the long apex area is almost eight car lengths. This turn happens to be an uphill right-hander that levels out at the end of the apex area but on the proper line for the entry. The car follows smoothly to the exit point.*

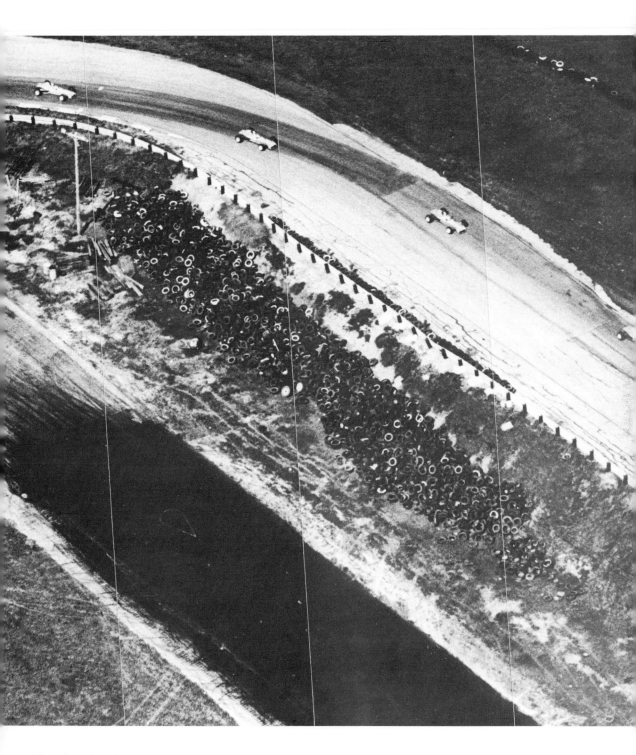

A long hairpin exiting and entering a straight-away. Note the late turn-in and the apex area three quarters of the way through the turn. A fast and easy long exit. No problems.

The same turn as before but here I turned in too soon, entered too early, apexed way too soon so the car drifted out too soon—the centrifugal force of cornering pushed the car to the outside and off course. If I had trail-braked to the middle of the turn I could have forced the car to stay inside and it could have been brought back to the proper exit line—slower, but safer than running off the road. This entry, if executed properly, could become a passing line but you have to get the exit right.

off your lap time. Think of it this way: All the turns do is tie the straight-aways together. The faster you can exit a turn, the faster you can get down the straight-away. The faster you can move down the straight-aways, the quicker you finish. Get the picture!

*When down-shifting, 5-4-3 versus 5-3 depends on the situation. One of the important factors to consider is that you make absolutely sure you have the proper rpm when you release the clutch if you've skipped a gear. If you go through all of them you shouldn't have that problem, but it's easy to have too many revs if you come down, say, from fourth to second without hitting third. Just be careful, save your equipment. The nature of the course can also make the decision for you. There's just a bit more margin and safety if, for example, you use all the gears if you have a wall nearby or no run-off area. If you have lots of run-off area or the barriers are set well back from the track then, sure, go ahead and go directly into the lower gear.*

*One thing I also might do is (if I'm really going in deep, when I'm passing from fourth to second) just pass through third gear; and if I feel like my braking is ok then I'll skip third and go on to second. It just gives a little margin for error if the braking isn't quite sufficient. I'd use third too, to put a little more weight on the rear wheels to help slow me some before second gear.*

Just don't forget to set up for and enter the corner properly to be able to have a faster exit. On the street you will want to approach the corner the same basic way except to make a more shallow entry. And remember, street apex areas are usually twice as long because the speeds are slower and the roads or lanes are narrower, minimizing the amount of road you have available to use. You really shouldn't be going the same speeds as on a racetrack anyway. But, if you get that urge, you had better be smooth and precise, have a good check in your mirrors, and know the area well. Most of all use your head, and be careful, if not for yourself, for the others on the road.

As far as the apex area goes, there is an early, middle and late apex. Each corner is slightly different, but as a rule, the apex area on the racetrack is usually about two thirds of the way around the corner. On the street, it will start in the middle and extend two thirds of the way around the corner.

The way to tell if you had the right apex or not is really simple. If you set up for the corner, and come out of it having to add more steering to keep from running off the road, then you had too early an apex. Or perhaps you hit the right apex but let the car drift out of the apex too soon. The same thing happens: You end up with not enough road. Your front tires will have to be turned to correct for your mistake and will slow you down. If you've picked too late an apex, then the car will be in too tight and you will not be able to drift the car to take full advantage of all the road. This is safer and ok for the street, but decidedly slower.

Ideally, you want to come out of the corner long and wide. If you are coming from a narrow road to a wide one, you will have an earlier apex because you will have more road to use when you exit. Just the opposite situation if you come from a wide road to a narrow one: you will have a very late and long apex.

Find a safe place to experiment and practice. Start slow and build up speed as you can handle it. Find out what happens if you apex early, late or properly; but do it where you won't damage your car if you go off the road. And, more importantly, where you won't hurt anyone else. That is one of the most important priorities of high performance driving. It is a responsibility. Use your head and good common sense.

At racing speeds it is very important to hit the proper apex. If you don't you'll find yourself off the road.

*I remember one time while I was tire testing for Goodyear. I was at Daytona in a Cobra and it was early morning, the car was warmed-up but I wasn't. With the Cobra, it first understeers badly, then it goes into oversteer as the power is applied, then it reaches a nice, smooth four-wheel drift. It feels great once you get the hang of it. But, this particular time, I was into the turn a little fast, didn't turn in quite as soon as I should have and all of a sudden I found myself sideways. Very embarrassing! Right in front of all the Goodyear people the first lap out the first day of a week of testing. I spun. God, did I spin! I went for a hell of a ride. I did two 360's off onto the grass. I hadn't set up right for the apex, so the centrifugal force took over and pushed me right off the track. I slid to a stop, put it in the proper gear and got going again. Simple as that. Had I been a little sharper, I would have turned in a little earlier and eased back on the throttle a little and saved it and a lot of embarrassment.*

Four-wheel drifts are lots of fun as witnessed here with one of my students in our Datsun Z school car. Like I said, use your head about when and where to take your car to the limit. . .keep the safety of others in mind when you practice.

That brings us to drifting, oversteer and understeer. Drifting through a corner means that all four wheels are sliding through the turn with the desired throttle control, making it nice and smooth. If the car is oversteering, the rear wheels are starting to slide. In understeer, the front wheels are starting to slide and the car won't go where you steer it.

You control the oversteer and understeer with the throttle and the steering, creating what is known as a four-wheel drift. Getting into a four-wheel drift is a lot of fun.

You can have power oversteer or simple oversteer. Power oversteer is when you come into the corner, set up trail-braking and let the rear end slide out a little, controlling it with the amount of throttle you feed it. Simple oversteer is a situation that usually indicates you're in trouble. You come into the corner braking too late, turn into the apex area with the front wheels sticking ok but the rear end is too light and you might lock up one or both rear tires. More often, when you don't keep enough throttle on while heel-and-toe downshifting, you'll momentarily lock up both rear wheels and go into a slide.

Sometimes you can still save it by easing in a bit of throttle which puts some weight transfer back to the rear wheels. Not a lot, or the turn is history! That's not a lot of fun. If you are in an oversteer situation and come off the throttle too quickly, the rear end of the car will be gone. It will come around on you so quickly you won't have time to correct with the steering.

*Practice different lines. Heavy traffic or other situations will often prevent you from being able to drive the ideal line through a corner. George Follmer (16) and I (93) are on the right line for this one at Riverside with a late apex area.*

Understeer is a situation in which you either turned in too early, at too high a rate of speed, or you got the throttle on too soon and too strong. If the latter was the case, too much weight was transferred *off* the front tires and they lost adhesion so the car wants to push you out of the turn. If you turn into the corner a bit early and go too fast to get to the apex area, the car is being pushed to the outside of the turn by inertia. You want to get the car into the apex area or you will run out of road at the exit. You add steering but the car is still heading to the outside. You are under throttle but the gear you are in doesn't have sufficient power to bring the rear end around enough to get you pointed right—the front wheels are still sliding. Here's what you do: Ease off the throttle; this will lighten the rear wheels and transfer some weight back to the front tires, the deflection of the sidewalls will scrub off some of your speed and give you back your steering. The rear end will come around now, changing the angle of the car. Correct as much as you need with the steering and ease back onto the throttle. The car will be stabilized again but you lost your speed advantage out of the turn because you had to get off the throttle due to a miscalculation. Down-shift and get going.

Practice, practice, practice! Learn your car and yourself! Take part in competitive activities that will get you to know what you and your car will do in any given situation. Slalom, autocross, etc.

*In a warm-up session, before a race ever starts, I will try different lines through different turns to see what will happen if I have to go there during the race. I want to have possibilities available to me, before I have to do it out of necessity. I want to know if I can pass someone on the inside or outside, going in or coming out of a given turn. I want to know if I can go high or low on a turn if there is someone spinning ahead of me. I want to know where I can go, safely, if I have to. That's just another aspect of knowing yourself, your car and the road around you. Experiment, find out what happens if you turn in too early, too late, or too deep. Find out what makes each apex area work in any kind of turn for you and your car. The kinds of turns are unlimited—increasing radius, decreasing radius, negative or positive camber, banked, hairpin, high-speed—each is different.*

*Every turn you approach will be different. There is no miracle formula that will teach you one standard way for every turn. The procedure, yes, but the line and apex area, no. It depends on you, your speed, your car and how that car is prepared. At the South African Grand Prix a couple of years ago, Desiré Wilson remarked how she had trouble there a few years earlier doing a corner flat-out in a Formula Ford; but in her Tyrrell Formula One car, flat-out (about 60 mph faster) was easy.*

*To learn to mathematically calculate your turns I strongly recommend that you read Taruffi's book* The Technique of Motor Racing. *Use his calculations as a base. Then use your head and work it out from there. On paper, turns can look simple and*

*Every corner has an entry, apex area and exit. This classroom session included Al Unser, Jr. (with Coke can), and fellow student Bill Mallery.*

*easy. The little figure in the drawing always makes it around the turn whether the diagram is correct or not. The photographs in this chapter of cars actually going through turns under power and loading is an attempt to give you some examples; but remember, your speed and your car (plus the amount of tire patch) and the way it is prepared will cause it to be slightly different. What we are giving you are the basics; the rest you'll have to find out from practice and experience. If you do find yourself getting into some trouble (almost everyone does sooner or later), then we're about to tell you how to (we hope) get out of it, or at least make it less of a problem.*

# CHAPTER NINE
# *Getting To Know Trouble*

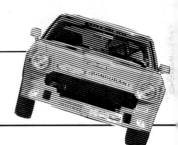

**N**o one wants to get into trouble but if you put many miles on a car, racing or on the street, you will inevitably be confronted by an emergency situation. This is where all that you have learned and trained for will come into play. You'll have to make a decision. . .quick! Your reactions will have to be lightning fast. You will only have a split second to do everything!

Basically there are two types of emergency situations: one that originates with you or your car and the other is a result of someone else's actions. The most common is one that occurs from you or your car, usually because you are careless or sloppy — not just in your driving but also in your car's upkeep and preparation. Maybe you lose a wheel, the throttle sticks or the brakes fail. . .you know, the usual things that can go wrong. There are a lot of things that can go wrong when you are driving. So, as we said before, do the best you can to maintain your car properly. If you do that, then the only thing you'll have to worry about is yourself. . .and the other guy who maybe doesn't care as much for his car or his driving technique.

As mentioned in the last chapter, if you are racing make sure that you try various lines in the corners to give yourself an option if something happens in front of you.

*At Monaco, in 1964, I was driving a Cooper Formula Three car for Ken Tyrrell that Jackie Stewart compaigned the year be- fore. I had set the fastest qualifying lap and was running well in* the race. I was just taking second place from Peter Revson. Monaco is really tight, even for Formula Three. To squeeze both of us through a turn I had to use every bit of the road. . .and a bit more. I had two wheels on the pavement and the other two on top of the hay bales at the edge of the road. I passed Peter and was so scared I didn't dare move the steering wheel or make any correction on the throttle. If I did I would go over the bales and into the bay. I didn't feel like going for a swim. So I smoothly and gently kept my steering and throttle just where they were and eased the car back down onto the road again. I completed my pass as I was coming down off the hay bales and into Tabac corner.

After I got by Peter, I had Roy Pike, the race leader, in my sights and decided I was going to catch him. There were only about six or eight laps left in the race and I finally caught up to him, and pressed him as hard as I could. He started driving harder and I was driving harder, too. For me to catch him meant I was obviously faster. If you are in the lead and all of a sudden there is someone out of nowhere on your tail you know he is a lot faster; so that really makes you try harder. In Roy's case, even though he was leading, the harder he drove the slower he went. . .remember, smooth is fast.

I wanted that lead. I had two spots picked out to pass him. One was out of the tunnel and the other was out of the Casino bend. As we headed up the hill to the Casino I was about two feet behind him and went into the corner as deep as I could, even over my head. He went in even deeper and I knew he wasn't going to make it. He didn't! He started to spin into the guardrail and I dove underneath him. What I hadn't counted on was, after he hit the guardrail he shot back across the track, right in front of me. Some choice I had: I could run right over the top of him or put my car sideways and spin myself. I put my car sideways and hit him wheel to wheel. That was the end of my right rear suspension. . .broken. And, for both of us it was the end of the race, on the last lap. Peter went by as we were climbing out of our cars and won the race. I should have used my head more. It was a two-heat race but because I was so determined to beat Roy Pike, I didn't make it to the second heat.

When I crashed, the first thing that I saw when I got out of the car was Fangio—Juan Manuel Fangio, the only five-time World Driving Champion. I had met him the day before and he had invited me to race in the Temporado series in Argentina, strictly an invitational series of races. And, here I am, crashed right in front of him. He was sitting on the veranda of the Hotel du Paris. I thought to myself, oh, my God, how embarrassing. That was the end of Monaco for me for that year.

That kind of thing can easily happen to anyone in a racing situation but it is unnecessary, and expensive. In racing once you've committed to a decision there's usually no second chance. Experience will help you to make the right decisions but getting that little bit of experience can at times be very costly. You must be sharp, alert and quick with the proper decisions. A moment's lapse of concentration and away you go.

Most out-of-control situations are a result of lack of concentration, trying to go too fast too soon, or simple carelessness. Sure, just doing something wrong, because you don't know better, happens also; but usually it's from driving over your head. If you're about to get into a situation that is going to be more demanding than you can handle, get out of it before you get into trouble. As your driving ability and experience become more complete you will be able to read a situation before it happens (in most cases).

*In the situation at Monaco, it was my first single-seater drive and the information I was acting on was from Corvettes and Cobras. I didn't realize that when a single-seater with open wheels hits a guardrail, the tires act like rubber bands and catapult the car right back into the way. The Corvettes just stayed put, usually.*

Most accidents and spins come from doing something wrong or doing nothing at all, rather than a wrong decision of where to go. Most of the time, a spin or accident can be avoided if you know what to do, which takes practice. Always remember to look where you want to go not where you are.

Now comes the hard part. Skid, slide, spin all mean you are out of control; or almost. We'll try to give you some control over them instead of just being a passenger and watching it all happen around you.

One of the first things that you probably were told when you started driving was if the rear end of your car starts to slide or skid,

*Notice, you turn the wheels in the direction of the skid. Along about this time you need to really have a fine touch on the throttle to keep it from coming on around. I can't emphasize too much the need for fast, fast reactions. I saved this one but it was almost to the point of no return. Notice how my head, although looking where I want to go, is only slightly tilted, keeping full body contact with the seat.*

turn your steering wheel in the direction the car is skidding. That's right; it works! How well it works is up to you. Your reactions have to be fast, very fast. . .lightning fast. Again you have to be in fine tune with your car and know as soon as the skid starts to happen how much to correct and when. The main thing is, *quickly,* as fast as you can, *move that wheel!* Immediately turn it in the same direction the rear end is starting to slide so you can start to stabilize the skid. If you react too slowly or turn the wheel too slowly or not far enough soon enough, you still might spin out.

There are a lot of different things that will make a surface slippery or slicker than normal: rain, snow, ice, other weather conditions, oil, gas, gravel, sand—with each you lose traction. The tires don't have enough adhesion and the car slides.

The most common skid that you will be confronted with is when the rear end slides out on you. Left or right, it's the same. Usually it has happened as a result of going into a turn too fast, or incorrectly, or hitting a slick area causing your rear wheels to oversteer. This can happen also from not adding enough throttle on a heel-and-toe down-shift causing the rear wheels to lock up, or putting on too much throttle in a turn before the direction and set of the car can handle it; or jumping on the brakes too hard, locking up the rear wheels. Whatever the cause, here's what to do.

*Stay off the brakes!* If you don't you might lose your steering. Then, *quickly,* steer in the direction that the rear of the car is sliding. If you still have on full throttle ease off enough to bring your wheels back into traction. Don't pull all the way off the throttle or it will take what weight you have on the rear wheels and move it forward, making the rear even lighter. In wet weather ease *all the way* off the throttle to lessen the skid or slide. If you caught the first slide, be ready for one in the other direction (caused by over-correcting). If it happens, adjust for the slide in the other direction. This, in a very fast situation, can happen back and forth several different times. Be ready each time and keep the car going in a forward motion or direction.

If the front end of the car is skidding in understeer, the correction to keep you from going off the road is simple but be careful because you may make it oversteer when you come out of the understeer condition. If the front end is pushing to the outside you will have to ease off the throttle to transfer the weight back to the front tires to gain steering control. The rear of the car should get lighter and your steering will come back; but the rear may then want to move out, so get ready to correct the steering in the same direction the rear end is sliding. If you can't correct your rear-wheel slide you will end up going the wrong way.

If you remember to look in the direction you want to go and steer in the direction you want to go, as quickly as possible, you will end up going in that direction. When the slide is corrected, straighten your steering wheel, fast! You easily know where straight ahead is because you always grab your steering wheel at three and nine so when your hands are there you should be going straight ahead.

When you make corrections in a skid make them quick and positive. Keep the car going in a forward direction and it doesn't usually matter if it takes one, two or three corrections to make it head in the right direction. If you are racing it makes a lot of difference in lap times, so try not to skid. Every time you have to correct in a major fashion, you are losing time. Being consistent and smooth saves time.

What if your car reaches an angle of ninety or more degrees to the direction you were traveling and it looks like you won't be able to catch the slide? Don't worry yet—you can, hopefully, still save the car, but the fast lap is now history. Again, *stay off the brakes!* What you want to do now is spin the car the rest of the way around and create a forward-180. This is where you are now traveling in the same direction as before but backward. Remember, the faster you are traveling the bigger the spin is going to be, and the faster you will have to try to correct it.

As soon as the car gets past ninety degrees (it's too late to keep it from spinning), straighten the wheel, put the clutch in and the gearshift in neutral. (If you don't keep the clutch in or put the car in neutral, the drive wheels will push against the directional movement of the car. That's a good way to flat-spot your tires, stall your engine and get into even more trouble.) You are still going in the same direction you originally were but now backward (a 180-degree spin). At this point there are two things you can do. One, carefully drive (back up) the car to a safe place to stop it; or two, spin it back around (if you have sufficient speed) and get going in the direction you had planned to go originally (a reverse 180-degree spin).

Neither maneuver is as difficult as it sounds. If you are heading backward down the track, watch your mirrors (remember, they should be adjusted properly) and steer the car where you want it to go. There is one slight catch: When you're going backward, the front wheel caster is reversed and your steering will be very quick. It's like backing out of a real long driveway, only at speed; very twitchy! You need to be very smooth and precise. Usually if you're in this kind of situation you have scrubbed off sufficient speed so you can now control the car easily. Ease on the brakes, slowing the car gradually. When you've come to a stop and are in a safe position on the road, turn back around, put it in gear and get going. If your car's broken and won't go any further and you are in a dangerous place just try to make sure it is sufficiently out of the line of traffic. Get out and become a spectator.

If you've still got sufficient speed while heading backward and have enough room to negotiate, without endangering someone else, then it's time to execute a reverse 180-degree spin. This is where you start out going backward and end up going forward. It's not difficult if you stay off the brakes. If you don't, you won't have enough speed to execute the maneuver.

*During training at the school, each maneuver is explained in detail then demonstrated before the student tries it. The same thing goes for a forward 180, reverse 180 and the combination of the two. We teach you behind-the-wheel, how-to-handle your car in these situations.*

So, here you are, heading backward at over 70 mph. What to do? While looking in your mirrors to see where you want to go, give the steering wheel a good crank, as fast as you can, snap-spin the wheel as fast as you can (no throttle or brakes) to complete full lock position. Turning the wheel either way will work. If there is another car or wall or barrier on one side of you, steer your rear end toward that and, since you're heading backward you'll spin in the other direction. The same as the forward-180, when the car gets past ninety degrees, straighten the wheel. . .you know, three and nine. When you straighten the wheel to go straight again it *must* be done fast and firmly.

Remember that during the whole procedure, the clutch is in and the car is in neutral, and the engine is kept running. While the car is coming around to straight ahead again, keep the clutch in but shift it to the gear that's going to handle the speed of your exit. That means you'll have to get your revs matched for your next exit speed just like a normal down-shift. As soon as you're heading in the right direction again ease out the clutch, ease on the throttle and away you go. The only time you need to alter this procedure is if the road is wet or you are on ice. Then, all you have to do is, after the car gets past ninety degrees, make sure you've turned to full lock. Hold it there and eventually (it seems like forever) it will come straight back around and you'll be going in the right direction. Remember, this is only on a wet and slippery surface with lots of room—*not on dry pavement*.

To do a 360-degree spin, you just combine a forward-180 and a reverse-180 and you'll be heading in the right direction if you're fast enough. It takes practice. . .like everything else. The best place to learn is on a skid pad. There you won't hurt yourself, your car or anyone else.

*At my school skid training is a very important part of the overall program and is found in each of my courses. The next step after skid control is accident avoidance. This is something I could have done better at Monaco, but maybe you'll learn from my miscalculation. The most important thing to understand is you can't stop as fast as you can avoid, especially at racing speeds. In the very first race in my Morgan at Santa Barbara, 1956, I was coming into turn nine at the old airport course and some guy in a Mercedes Gullwing lost it right in front of me. First race. . .great! Right in front of me. I swerved to miss him and ended up spinning myself. Everyone said, "Oh, wow, you did great; a great job spinning to miss that guy." The fact of the matter was I really didn't try to spin, all I wanted to do was miss him. Well, I missed him.*

*That was my very first incident in a race. There have been more but through experience I learned how to avoid a problem, usually without having to spin to avoid it. On many occasions I've had to swerve to miss other people spinning or to miss oil dropped from a blown engine or whatever. It can be done safely and usually without incident if you are really alert and your reactions are fast enough. Here we are again, right back to concentration, alertness, anticipation and reaction speed—everything that you have if you are physically and mentally fit.*

Avoidance is usually quite easy. Someone spinning in front of you is a typical situation on a race circuit. On the street it may be a child's ball or a dog running in front of you that must be avoided. First, *don't use your brakes.* Come off the throttle, immediately. This transfers the car's weight and momentum forward giving you a larger tire patch at the front. Second, steer to avoid the object. At speed, a slight turn is enough then immediately correct to your forward direction and feed in the throttle.

Object past. Where to steer to? It depends on what you are avoiding but in the case of a spinning race car the best place to head for is where it has already been. That's to say if the car in front of you spun left and hit the wall it will go to the right in front of you; so, head where the car already has been, to the left. In a real high-speed situation you'll have to be faster than you can imagine. If you stay off the throttle too long in an avoidance manuever, the rear end will get light and you can spin too. Therefore it's really important to get the power back on as soon as you can see that you are going to miss what's in front of you.

If you can't avoid the object and you are forced to stop, make sure your wheel is turned straight ahead. Get ready. . .we are about to stop. . .fast. . .Panic City! If there is no place to go and it's either stop or crash then you'd better know how to stop. Simple term number thirty thousand (at least your mind is getting a workout) : *ca-*

*Skid control; an essential part of the total high performance program. I use it in the "Corporate Course" and the Law Enforcement Academy, too. It's amazing what you can learn on a skid pad, about your car and yourself.*

dence brake. Nice word? Nice procedure. It is the only thing that might stop you. And there is no guarantee, it depends on how fast you are going and how much distance you have in which to stop.

Procedure. . .especially in wet weather, but it works in the dry too. Very simple. Your foot comes off the gas, weight transfers to the front, increasing the tire patch. If you ease on the brakes like a normal braking situation you won't have time to stop. If you panic and use the "Oh, shit" method and lock your brakes, you've lost your steering *and* your traction so you'll slide right into what you're trying to avoid. Using cadence braking you'll stop in half the distance.

Here's how it goes: Put the brakes on full, just to the locking point, then rapidly come clear off them, then on again full, then off again full, on, off, on, off, rapidly. . .very rapidly. The faster you can pump them on and off, the faster the car will stop. It takes some practice but it works if you do it fast enough. Pump them as fast as you can on and off till the car comes to a stop.

You might want to change direction somewhat as you are slowing. Here's how: Come completely off the brakes for an instant, make your steering correction, straighten the wheel again then continue cadence braking till stopped. If, for some reason, you are in a full locked braking situation, which you shouldn't be but you are, and you must change your direction slightly (say, if you are on ice), come off the brake, make your steering adjustment and then cadence brake—don't just hold the pedal to the floor.

The key is to feel everything your car is doing and anticipate what might happen in any given situation or road condition. Be ready for it to happen because when it does you aren't going to have much time to make more than one decision. Practice, practice, practice. . .Find somewhere safe like a vacant parking lot, and see what your car does.

*OK, here's what you've been waiting for, a plug for the school. It takes practice on a skid pad to find out what it really takes to cadence brake, correct massive oversteer, spin 180 and 360 degrees and the like, safely. My school has skid-control instruction. Most of the other driving schools don't. Some think that it's unnecessary, others just don't have the facilities or the room available. It is, however, really an important step to learning complete car control. You have to know what you and your car will do when the situation presents itself.*

Adverse weather conditions present even greater hazards and the need for even greater smoothness and concentration. In the rain, a typical turn can become an instant nightmare if overdone. Your line through a turn in the rain will start a little sooner and slower for a shallow entry. Your apex area might be twice as long and low or higher and just a bit above the normal racing line because in the rain that's where the traction is. You have to judge the shape and type of turn and you'd better get it right. Where the rubber has been placed on the track will become more slippery than where there is no rubber. So, where you have the greatest traction in the dry, from rubber build-up, the opposite happens in the rain. You want to have a higher, more stable and smoother line. You may even have to straddle the rubber that has been laid down, sometimes higher or lower because of puddles. Question: Why? Answer: Maximum traction!

Good anticipation comes from experience and learning to watch the other driver. First, be in control of yourself, then watch the people you're coming up on, then get familiar with them. Not just on the racetrack or driving but get to know them personally too and you get to know their different personality traits that could help you on the circuit. Experience is learning to read other people too. Learning their moves and seeing what they do and how they handle themselves in a variety of situations. The same goes for traffic, passing and drafting. Look far enough ahead to judge and get to know your competition, keep alert and anticipate. With experience you should be able to take it all in and make the correct decisions. Each circumstance is different—but learn from watching. Just because the driver in front of you gets the passing flag don't expect him to pull off the road to let you by. It depends on the driver, so you may get plenty of room or may have to race to pass.

That's where experience and how well you learn to read your competition come in handy. The driver might make it look like you are getting a lot of room then slam the door on you. Just keep alert and watch everybody. It's a lot better to profit from someone else's mistake than from your own. Traffic, and passing are nothing more than mental gymnastics. Everyone is trying to psych out the other guy.

*One important thing you need to learn in racing is the ability to anticipate when someone in front of you may be getting into trouble—especially important when following a competitor closely. Stay alert, always! And look well ahead, too.*

Drafting: You can pick up a draft at least six to eight car lengths behind the car in front of you. The closer you get the easier it is to run faster. You are in what is referred to as his "slipstream." This makes both cars run faster than if there was just one car cutting through the air; but there are problems, too. A good example of drafting can be seen at any NASCAR race with the leaders usually running nose to tail. They run faster but the second car has a real problem with cooling if they run that way too long. The lead car has a problem too, as the second car can easily whip out from behind and gain momentum and pass the leader with ease. In many of the races now, especially with ground-effects cars, it is extremely difficult to drive close to the car in front due to the turbulence created by the extreme downforce. The turbulence can cause both the car in the front and the car in the rear to become unstable. Running in close company has resulted in some of the Formula One cars recently having had wings ripped off by the turbulence. Know what your car will do in all situations.

In traffic you need to have a plan to get through. You're going to have to make your plans and decisions quick; but once you do, you're committed so it better be the right decision. After you get by one car forget about that one and start concentrating on the next. . .How you're going to get by and where. . .Plan, think and be quick and decisive. And, watch what's happening. . .look for weaknesses — that goes for the car and the driver.

You now know that everything that you do in a car must be smooth. When braking or accelerating, it must be eased into and out of. In rain or other adverse conditions you can multiply that about five times. If you aren't smooth you are off the road. When you drive in adverse weather you must be more alert, and every little thing that you do must be smooth and precise. You will be going decidedly slower in the rain or you will be off the road.

When you do go off the road the most important thing to do is to turn the wheels straight the instant just before you leave the road so you don't dig a wheel into the dirt and flip over. The next most important thing is to not hit anything. Assuming that you don't have a problem with that, the next most important thing is to either stop or get back on the road. Let's say that you don't need to stop because all that happened was you apexed too early and you ran out of pavement at the exit, putting two wheels off the road. There is no real problem if the shoulder will support you and the edge of the road is absolutely even, without a lip. Ease off the throttle slightly and hold your line. Don't try to steer immediately back onto the pavement or you could dig a wheel into the edge of the pavement and either spin or roll the car when attempting to come back on the road.

Again, like most situations: *Stay off the brake!* Hold your line, maintain your traction and ease smoothly and slowly back onto the road surface. The same thing goes for having all four wheels off course — ease back on where you can safely. If there is a grass surface at the edge of the road be prepared to quickly correct any oversteer that might follow and be ready to ease back on the throttle a little if your tires lose traction. But. . .stay off the brakes!

The above-mentioned procedures will work with almost all cars except front-wheel-drive vehicles. Here you have more weight over the front wheels, increasing the front tire patches, but less weight at the rear and possibly less available traction at the rear.

Cornering techniques as well as oversteer and understeer characteristics are slightly different. Front-wheel-drive cars have power understeer with the front wheels (the ones that you steer with). . . interesting concept? And different. You brake, enter the turn in a normal way, down-shift then trail-brake into the turn. You *must* ease off the brake or the inside rear wheel (probably off the ground) will lock and make the already light rear end want to swing around even more (remember, this is still oversteer). This puts an even greater load on your outside front wheel. If the rear starts to come around

*Rain causes the track surface to be especially slippery. With the horsepower and handling of a 427 Cobra you had to be forcefully gentle, with a very light touch and feel to control the car in the rain.*

you must *accelerate* to *pull* yourself out of the corner. The acceleration transfers the weight again to the rear and increases the traction.

So far, so good, but if you put in full throttle to save the back end you might lose the front. The car might go into understeer (maybe power understeer) and the front will, even with acceleration and steering correction, push to the outside. Most of the weight is on the front and it will be actually forcing the tires to lose adhesion. What you must do if the front end starts to go is. . .you know, stay off the brake. In this case, you have a throttle problem too.

If you come off the throttle all the way both the front and the rear will lose traction and you'll be gone. If you stay on the throttle the front will completely wash out. . .What to do?. . .Prayers help, but if you don't have time, come off the throttle quickly, then depress it again just as quickly, on/off, on/off, just like cadence braking. This will get you through the turn, a bit jerky, but through it. It looks funny and your friends will be laughing but you'll make it through the corner. But don't try to corner this way in each turn. It's not the fastest way. One more time, do it right and maximize traction. Cadence throttle. . .front-wheel-drive only. It can get you out of trouble.

*A typical front-wheel-drive entering a corner (not trail-braking—no brake lights). Weight is shifted forward and to outside front. Note the patch area of all tires in this situation.*

# CHAPTER TEN
## Getting Into Racing

**A**way we go into the never-never-land of buying a race car. Stop! Wait a minute! Is that really what you want? Ask yourself a few questions before you take that big and very expensive step. Do you really have what it takes?. . .time?. . .talent?. . .determination? and . . .lots of money?

How do you know you are even going to like racing? Have you ever driven a car to its limit? Are you going to panic the first time it gets sideways?. . .good possibility. Let's put it this way: Do you want to spend $10,000 on a car that's going to scare you to death? Or, maybe driving around by yourself is ok but you nearly run off of the road to get out of the way of someone passing you. Don't like traffic? How do you find out till you try it? And, how do you try it without buying a car? Please read on.

One of the fastest and cheapest ways to learn if you like driving a car fast and to find out if you might make a good race driver is to take a high performance/racing course at a nationally respected driving school. This first investment can either stop a career before it ever starts, or get it headed in the right direction with a minimum cost. At this point, don't waste money on a car. Invest it in *yourself*. You'll have more to show for it. Racing is *not* like driving fast on the road. Not even close! It doesn't matter how closely you follow the sport or how sure you are that you want to race, until you try it you'll never really know what it's like. People can tell you what it is like but

*Give yourself the best possible chance of becoming a successful race car driver; start out with the instruction offered by a professional driving school. Here Bobby Unser, Jr., and I are discussing driving techniques during an advanced instruction session.*

until you try it for yourself you'll never know. You may even surprise yourself and be better than you think.

Racing is very expensive, there is a lot to learn and it can be dangerous, so get the best training and the most experience you can before you ever think about buying a car. Attending driving schools is the least expensive way to learn how to drive a race car. Most schools will teach you the proper way to do things, on an individual basis, before you have a chance to learn the "traditional way" of doing them wrong. The traditional way, trial and error, can be costly and not very gratifying. It causes a lot of very potentially talented drivers to fall by the wayside. Sometimes it is money, disappointment in the car they bought, or just not being able to get around a turn properly (which could be the car too). Whatever, many are lost without really giving themselves a fair chance. Try a school first. Prepare *yourself* before you ever think about buying a race car or converting your street car; enroll in a school. It's also an ideal way of picking up advice as to the best way to start racing.

It will take a lot more time and money to reach the same level of driving expertise by the trial and error method than by proper school training and instruction. Many trial and error drivers *never* reach the proficiency of the school graduate. Any racing school is better than none, but if you are really serious you might want to try a couple of different schools before you embark on that long and expensive road of race car ownership.

*I feel that the Bondurant school offers the most complete and thorough instruction. You want to be sure that you attend a school that will provide you with the most firm foundation possible. The Bondurant school is the only school that progresses from Datsun sedans to two-seater Datsun Z sports cars, then to single-seater For-*

mula Ford race cars. I believe that learning students must have an instructor riding with them (as at the Bondurant school) to see exactly what mistakes are made and get them corrected immediately. It is also necessary to ride with an instructor to see exactly what that instructor really does—not just what he might say. You'll see the proper use of hands on the wheel, good feet position on the pedals, heel-and-toe down-shifting, trail-braking and proper seating position. From them you will learn to use your eyes better and look way ahead. To see the turn properly and what the road ahead is like, especially with other cars on it, are all important.

From there I do recommend that you, providing that you still want to race, try other schools as well. Most of the other schools are geared in the direction of Formula Ford. My school has that as part of the total program, but many of the other schools now sponsor racing series. These series provide you with a car (well prepared), actual racing time and competition. Your investment is your time and a minimal amount of money—far less than if you had to buy and field your own car. If, after a few races you feel that this isn't quite what you wanted, you can just walk away. You won't have the worry of your own car (that probably didn't work right anyway) that you have to get rid of, probably at a loss.

The instruction and its completeness varies a bit from school to school but you will get what you pay for. In some cases a lot more. How much you learn and how well you learn is up to the instructor, the school's basics and you. If you don't follow the instructions given you, and lots of times it's easier not to, you are cheating only yourself. Go to a driving school with the attitude that you are going to learn all that the instructors can possibly teach you, and you'll do well. It's not a vacation or going around the track in a parade—it's serious business. It's work, but it can also be very satisfying.

OK, let's assume that you've gone to a racing school, or better yet a couple of them, competed in a series and decided that you want to be a road racer. Now what? Yes, you might want to buy a car, but also you might try to put together a whole package at once. What you need first is a license. SCCA (Sports Car Club of America) or

*To familiarize students with the circuit they take several laps behind an instructor (in Datsun sedan). They take note of his racing line through turns. Then the instructor follows the student, taking note of what the student is doing. After this session they stop and go over everything.*

*Students in my school start out in Datsun sedans then move into the faster, more responsive Datsun Z sports cars before they get to the Formula Fords.*

*After you've mastered the "Z's" you're moved up to the Formula Fords. Crawling into the narrow cockpit of one of these babies—your eyes about level with the tops of the tires—is a real thrill for my students and it's still even fun for me, too.*

IMSA (International Motor Sports Association)? What kind of racing do you want to do? How much money do you have? Until you've done some racing you probably won't find a sponsor; so guess who is going to foot the bills? Right, *you!* So, let's get the most for your money.

Just because you don't have a car yet doesn't mean that you can't go to SCCA schools. You might have a friend who will loan you his car or maybe you can rent one for the weekend (still a cheaper investment). For information on all the current requirements and fees you should contact the SCCA. That organization will also be able to inform you when there will be an SCCA driving school in your region. To get a novice license you must satisfactorily complete two SCCA driver's schools or one SCCA driver's school and one private competition school. For full and current details you'd be wise to contact the club. Things change, so keep current.

In IMSA, you are eligible for a provisional license after satisfactorily completing an approved competition driving school course. Again, contact IMSA directly for the most current regulations on its licensing.

*You'll want to find out all of the rules and classes available in both sanctioning groups so let's get the legwork started. I know, I know! You want to get to the good part. . .buying a car. Hold on. We're just about there. Don't forget, you are learning! So, listen, take a deep breath and hold on. Here we go!*

*Time. . .* Take your time. There's not the rush that you think. We've already established that it's better to ease into things than jump into full throttle right away, so why would it be different with buying a race car? It's not. Chances are that you're going to have to wait for a school anyway. Make use of your time to observe. You probably have picked out a class that either fits your pocketbook, your self image or both.

Place your priorities where they belong; reliability and affordability. Use your head, take your time and be sure of what you are getting. *Reliability is a must.* You have to be able to concentrate on your driving to do well, so make sure you buy a car that you aren't going to have to worry about keeping together. Both reliability and affordability are going to be determining factors in what you end up buying but you had better put that together with common sense too. Forget about, for now at least, the high-priced formulas and the super-fast racers — they will not help you learn.

A super-fast car is too damn dangerous for learning, it is usually very unforgiving. By super-fast we mean Atlantic, Can-Am, Turbo Porsches. These, for most, are out of the question from the affordability standpoint but some think they should start at the top if they have the money to do so. Forget it! Start in a smaller, less-powerful car. Find out what you are doing with a car you can handle. You should have a good deal of respect for a race car but you shouldn't be afraid of it. Start out with a car that you can feel comfortable in and that you think you can master and explore its limits. Then you will be learning. Field a first-class effort in whatever class you can afford. It's better to have a first-class Showroom Stock Rabbit than a bare-boned Super-Vee with no spare parts. You can move into the faster cars after you master the slower ones.

Maybe after attending a racing school you have decided that Formula Ford is for you. That's a good choice, especially if you have aspirations of becoming professional. It is extremely competitive, and in many areas there are pro race series. The Fords are also very popular so you'll learn how to race wheel-to-wheel. Fords are fast without being ridiculous for the beginner, and they are both sophisticated and reasonably affordable. If you decide to go in that direction you will learn a lot about driving, racing and chassis set-up.

Maybe a fifty-car field isn't quite what you had in mind. Maybe the open wheels scare you. Maybe racing will scare you no matter what you are driving. . .one more reason to start out with something you can handle. If racing scares you too much, then you probably aren't going to make it, so you aren't going to be looking for a car to buy. But if racing scares you just a little—join the crowd! There are times that anyone is going to be scared—out around the limit of traction, for instance. If you are going to be successful then you are going to find out about *your* limits, your *car's* limits and your *tires'* limits. When you do you'll be over your head, you'll slide, you'll spin (maybe even crash) and you'll go right back for more. It'll take "Balls." Balls by themselves won't get you any place but in the hospital, but combine that extra bit of daring and you've just discovered one more bit of necessary character that will make you a successful racing driver. If you aren't scaring yourself a bit at the limit then you're probably going too slow. Back to the car.

If you have decided that you want to start in one of the production categories. . .Great! On the regional level there can be good competition and it is relatively inexpensive. Showroom Stock is the least expensive way to start and is good experience. One important word on this: If you are considering making your own sports car into a race car, *forget it!* It is ridiculously expensive, time-consuming and probably one of the worst investments you could make. You will put much more time and money into converting your car than if you buy one ready to race. "Ready to race," that has a nice ring to it. It does if it is indeed ready to race. Unfortunately most used racing cars aren't. Not all, but most. We'll forego the horror stories. You'll get to hear enough of them talking to your racing buddies.

*SCCA club racing fields an interesting mix of cars.*

This is why we've been taking the time to observe. You've been going to races, deciding what class you want to run in and you've been watching and sizing-up your future competition. In the class that you have chosen you have been studying all the cars, drivers and teams. You should know which ones are good, fast and reliable. You have decided to buy one of them. You talk to, say, the owner who qualified his car for the regional (or national) run-offs. The car is fast and reliable, it's been driven well and the upkeep has been meticulous. He will sell you the car as soon as the season's over. But he wants to clean it up and make sure it's in good order after the last race. *Wrong!* When he gets out of the car at the end of its last race, take delivery on the spot. That's your insurance you'll have all the goodies you are paying for.

This process of picking out what car to get is the real problem. Invest six months or so going to a lot of races at different circuits. Talk to the competitors about their cars and others. Keep your eyes open and look. Watch how they drive, how they work on their cars, how they repair them and how clean they keep them. Look for a driver who respects his car, tools and equipment. Look for the smooth driver who has the proper tools to care for his car — that's who to buy from. It's a good idea to take along someone who knows the cars and classes or a good racing mechanic to look at a potential car when you get to the point of really serious buying. Go to the owner's workshop and look the car over carefully. If the car doesn't have good paint, interior, a sanitary engine and good clean wiring then the car is probably deficient in a lot of other areas too. Let the buyer beware.

A serious and meticulous owner will have complete records on the car. Every race and testing lap that the car has run should have been recorded along with modifications, gearing and speeds. Don't take everything that the owner says for fact. Ask for proof. If he is honest he will have no objections. Ask to see his receipts; they tell a lot. Look over his workshop. Is it clean, well-equipped? Take a look at the person selling the car. Would you want to buy a used car from him? Or better still, would you want him to work on your race car? You'd better come up with the right answer to that one. . .he's been working on it for at least the last season.

Take your time. There are a lot of race cars out there and if one gets away there will always be another. Don't rush into something that you might regret later. Find the right one. There's one more little detail that you'll have to take care of if you're going to race: safety equipment. Get the best you can afford; it can save your life. Don't cut corners here — the better-quality equipment lasts longer, is safer and offers the best protection. Before you buy anything see what the other drivers (top drivers) are wearing. Find out what the SCCA and IMSA have on their approved list.

*I recommend one-piece driving suits, and full-face-type helmets with nomex hoods. The more protection you can give your-*

*One kind fits all. . .guys and gals.*

*self the safer you'll be. In an enclosed car the open-faced helmets are still approved but a full-face, Bellstar M-1 type is much safer—especially in the case of fire. Again, the more you're protected the more you can concentrate on driving. Safe is sane, don't cut corners on safety equipment—buy the best.*

More to think about? Don't worry, this is just the start. Once you get your race car you'll really have a lot to think about. Have you made any decisions yet? Made a deal to buy a car? Which one? This season's regional E production champion after he runs it at the national run-offs in Atlanta? Picking it up on the spot? Right, you've been listening. It sounds like you're really getting into this in a big way. How about what we just talked about? You've already enrolled in the Bondurant school for starters then Bertil Roos' then Skip Barber's school and racing series. By that time you should have your car after the run-offs and will have the whole winter to prepare and test it. Very important, testing and practice. Especially with a new car. There are a lot of other things you can do too, so keep reading. Glad to hear you're putting it all together.

# CHAPTER ELEVEN
## *Getting A Sponsor*

*L*et's assume your basic training was a success, you bought a reliable competitive car and have a season or two behind you with lots of victories. All your friends say, "You should be a pro." If you do aspire to be a professional racer then you had better get the idea planted firmly in your mind that *it is serious business!* If you think it's not then you are seriously mistaken.

The successful professional racer and successful business person have a lot in common. What does it take to be successful? These attributes apply to both: Well organized. Aggressive. Persistent. Competitive. Confident. Success oriented. Egotistical. Self-centered. And a very positive attitude. Just the kind of guy you'd want your sister to marry? Not fantastically flattering but to the point. Of course, not all successful business people would make successful racers, but these days to be a successful racer you *must* be or become business oriented.

If you are serious about racing as a full-time career then you've just started to learn about what it takes. How you handle yourself off the track can be just as important as how you handle yourself on it. You must now learn how to be a PR person. You need to be able to handle yourself well with the press, your sponsors, potential sponsors, car owners, crew, track personnel and everyone else concerned with racing. You must give the media good interviews and learn how to provide your sponsors the best coverage (diplomatically) in all your

*Let your enthusiasm for racing show.*

interviews—press, radio as well as television! Perhaps the most important ingredients to your success (besides good driving) are good attitude, honesty and a pleasant personality. Be yourself, and true to what you believe. You have to live with yourself first so use integrity and you'll get along better with everyone else, too. A really important thing is to show all that great enthusiasm you have. It's good for the media, your sponsors, racing and you. Some people hold it in. . .don't. . .Let it show! You'll get better coverage if you show it. That's what can make you or break you. . .that and cooperation. Don't become a braggart—remember actions speak louder than words! It's a job, so work at it.

If you are really serious about your racing you're going to find that it takes more than desire, talent and enthusiasm. Pro or amateur, it takes a lot of money too. There aren't many of the "gentleman racers" left who have huge fortunes to spend on racing. Today, most first-class efforts are the result of sponsors and advertising. There's an old joke about how you can make a small fortune in racing: Start with a large one. Unfortunately in the current racing market, that is about the size of it. As racing becomes increasingly more expensive each season, the need for a driver to sell himself, his talent and his racing program to a sponsor or sponsors is greater than ever.

You'll want to keep up on what's happening in the business world too. That's the only way you can make realistic proposals to sponsors. Find out what the sponsors' market needs are and try to fulfill them. Get familiar with *The Wall Street Journal, Business Week,*

*Entrepreneur* and the like. You'll really never know where a sponsor might come from. Some do it for the direct marketing advertising. For others it's simply a way to entertain clients and friends.

For an independent to run in anything beyond a club-type program without any sponsorship, and be competitive, is not too likely in these times. You must have a good understanding of corporate needs, advertising and business practices as well as being able to *effectively present* and *communicate* to your sponsor. Just being a good driver doesn't cut it anymore. Sad but true. Look at Formula One, you can count on your fingers the number of drivers who didn't have to buy their rides. The same thing goes for club racing. . .only it's *you* who puts the money up for yourself and your car.

If you find a sponsor you are the lucky one. Help that person or company in any way you can. Give your sponsor his money's worth. Don't just take the dough and ask for more when it runs out. There probably won't be more if you don't work with your sponsor. This goes right up the line all the way to Formula One. It may require personal appearances, talk shows, radio, car shows, whatever. Maybe photos and personal meetings with your sponsor's friends or business contacts at a race meet, whatever. . .do it.

If you don't have the time or know how to find a sponsor, then hire a good public relations firm. But remember, you still have to do your part to keep the sponsor happy.

*A well-heeled effort often requires the product and/or cash assistance of several sponsors—there are about a dozen logos displayed on this Porsche 935 I co-drove to third place at Sebring in 1979.*

*Don't let promotion work get you down; it can be a lot of fun too. That's me, without the bunny ears and tail, while on a Shelby PR tour in St. Louis.*

In a recent Formula One season the then reigning World Champion had a contract with a camera company that was very active in Formula One. He took the money but found little time for the sponsor. The sponsor felt slighted, rightfully so, and cut back all of its racing program. This affected far more than just the one selfish and thoughtless driver. The "It's not my problem" attitude affects all involved in racing. Just don't forget, a good, friendly, positive and cooperative attitude goes a long way. A sponsor lost is usually one that is not regained. . .usually ever, by anyone. Burned once, twice shy! End of lecture. . .Just remember, if you find someone who has the faith in you to help you, give them the help they need in return.

# CHAPTER TWELVE
## Take Some Tips From Me

*You've been preparing your mind, your body and your car, so what's next? Practice, practice, practice! The schools helped, the school racing series gave you an idea what competition is like. You've bought a good car and now you have to learn about it. Remember: safety, reliability, then performance, in that order. Now that it's time to practice, here are a few bits of information to help you on your way.*

*First, there is no such thing as too much practice. Unfortunately when you're talking about practice you're also talking about a lot of time and money. Practice doesn't mean just driving around the track. That's what a lot of people do but that's not what I'm talking about. The quality of time spent practicing is perhaps more important than the amount of time spent. Make each lap count. Really concentrate and feel exactly what your car is doing.*

*Most tracks are available to groups or individuals to rent, but it's expensive, so spend your time fruitfully. Don't pay your practice fee and sit there working all day long on the car, hardly turning a wheel. Work on your car in the garage so you don't waste your money. Arrive at the track with your car well-prepared and ready to race. . .Just like a race weekend!*

*Before you even think about going to a track to practice have in mind what you want to work on and accomplish. Do you want to improve a basic or a special technique, your car's handling, see how a new bit does or doesn't work? Know what you want to do. Every lap costs you money in, if nothing else, car and tire wear. So, make sure you are going to get your money's worth.*

*Preparation is the key to both successful practice and successful racing. Your car must be meticulously prepared and be as safe as theoretically possible to enable you to get the most out of your practice, testing, qualifying or racing. Don't make excuses to yourself why you can't do something. Just do it or don't run. There is actually one little step past preparation that will really make a difference as to how both you and your car perform: warm-up. It's an absolute necessity. An athlete, say a runner, wouldn't consider starting a race cold. He'd injure himself, strain something and just wouldn't perform up to what he could if all of his muscles were warm and ready to go.*

*The same thing applies to a car, on the street or track. Warm-up is imperative. By this I don't just mean let the car idle for a few minutes then take off and drive hard. By warm-up I mean a complete warm-up. Think of it like this: In the morning when you first wake up you might be a little slow and sluggish till you have your morning exercise or coffee or whatever. It takes a few minutes to get yourself going, before you're functioning up to par. Your car has to wake up gradually, too. There are parts that take a little more time to get ready to go than others. The engine is usually the first thing to warm up. But then what? You probably haven't even thought about it. Now's the time.*

*Warm the engine at a medium idle before you do anything else. This will give you a bit of time to think, relax and plan before you get underway. When the water temperature moves into the operating range you're ready to start out. Don't forget, right now the only thing that's warmed up is the engine so take it easy.*

*Many students bring their own cars for my course—this one is way too wide of the apex area which is marked by pylons.*

The wheel bearings, transmission, differential oil and the gears are all still cold. Take it easy on the track, give it a couple of laps at a slow speed. On the street, give your car a couple of miles to get everything warm. Getting all the running parts warmed up will cut the wear and increase the life of your car. You'll have fewer failures and it will perform better for a longer period of time. For peak performance both you and your car need that extra little bit of easy warm-up (sort of like foreplay). Just give yourself that few extra minutes for preparation, it'll maximize your potential and in the long run everything will work better, longer. Don't forget, racetrack or street, high performance driving is knowing what you and your car are doing all of the time.

Be sure that the running gear, shock absorbers and tires are warmed up too. The tires are, for safety reasons, the most important things to have up to working temperature. If they're not warm enough before you really get into it then there is little adhesion. . .into the weeds! A formula car will take a little longer to warm up than a sedan or sports car simply because it weighs less. Also, the harder the tire compound, the slower it is to warm up. And if the temperature is really cold or the track damp it will take even longer to bring your tires up to optimum operating temperature, maybe a couple of laps—so don't rush it.

What about tires. . .all of the manufacturers claim theirs are best, so what are you going to choose? If you are asking about a street car, showroom stocker or IMSA radial sedan racer then you've got many to choose from. Read the reports in Road & Track, Car and Driver, Motor Trend and the like. Also, talk to people with the same kind of car. Try to drive several cars to find out what the different tires are like. Your dilemma then becomes a process of elimination.

For racing in the US, the novice or national racer is probably best off with Goodyear. That's what most of the competition will be using. If you're running the same tires as your competition and they are just as new then you've just eliminated a variable in how your car handles in comparison to the competition. The more variables you can eliminate the quicker you'll be able to set up and dial in your car. For the proper rates of inflation, check with your tire representative at the event—one more reason for Goodyear.

Tire temperatures should be monitored every time you come into the pits. It will give you a definite clue as to what your car is or isn't doing and your tire rep will be able to tell you how and where to check the temps and what they mean. The inflation rates and types of compounds to use on a given day are other bits of information your tire rep can give you. They will be of as much help as possible since it's to their advantage to see you do well. That's what they're there for and part of what you paid for when you bought those expensive skins. The same goes for wet weather *tires. Talk to your rep and use the information that is available to you.*

*For the street, tire choices are numerous. As I said, do your homework, research. What kind of tread? What kind of tire? The technology of tire development is changing constantly. There will always be better and stickier tires, for the street or the track. Keep on top of it by listening, researching and, if possible, testing. Tire wear and tire life are a definite consideration if you are on a very limited budget. Bandag retreads last about four times longer than regular street tires and will actually give you comparatively faster lap times. I use them on all my school cars, and on my Datsun Z's they are about three-seconds-a-lap faster than street tires. (By the way, Bandag retreads can be put on any good tire carcass such as Goodyear Eagles or NCT's, Pirelli P-7's, Michelin, Goodrich, Firestone or any other regular street tire.) In my school I have used Bandag recaps on both street tires and on Goodyear racing tires for over six years with absolutely no problems and great results. I've even raced on their racing recaps at Daytona (twenty-four hours) and Sebring (twelve hours) at speeds slightly over 150 mph.*

*For the street, or showroom stock racing, tire pressures are really important. Keep your tires properly inflated. I recommend between thirty-two and thirty-four pounds. If you intend to drive your high performance car fast or hard, then you'd better push your tire pressures a bit above the manufacturer's recommended pressures. At my school I run all of the cars with thirty-four psi all the way around. It's a real safety factor. When street tires (on most street wheels) are run at or below normal inflation rates the tire bead can break under hard cornering, the tire can roll over and come off the rim. If it comes off while you're really pushing hard in a corner, the wheel rim edge will dig into the pavement and you could be in for a big accident, maybe even a roll-over. Like the rest of your car, keep the tires in top condition and properly inflated. They're your only contact with the road surface—keep it that way. If you have treaded tires, make sure you have enough tread. Whether race or street tires, be sure too that they are in proper balance. Not only will you prolong their life but you won't have high-speed vibrations from them and you'll greatly reduce your chances of over-heating and blistering them and having a blow-out as a result.*

*In addition to concern about your tires should be thoughts about your shock absorbers and anti-sway bars. At my school I use Kontrolle shocks, and Quickor springs and sway bars. There are many kinds of shocks and anti-sway bars available on the market. What kind you get, what's the best for your car and what kind lasts longest can be as confusing as what kind of street tire to buy. Your car's handling will be improved by aftermarket shocks and sway bars, so you'll have to do some research again. Find out* what's available, ask a lot of questions and do your research to determine the best choice for your car. Suspension specialists like Quickor can give you the best set-up for the kind of driving that you want to do with your particular car. Each kind of driving has different handling requirements. Setting up your car for the street is different from a slalom, autocross, rally or modified production racing set-up. Each requires a different kind of suspension setting so you'd be best off to contact a suspension specialist, like Quickor or Kontrolle, to design one for your car and your needs.

Back to the track; once you've decided on the specific areas you want to work on and properly warmed up your car and tires, you should pick a predetermined engine red-line and stick to it. This should remain constant so you can gauge improvement accordingly. Pick a high enough red-line so you can run fast enough to find out what the car will do and spot changes, but also be sure to pick a red-line that won't blow your engine.

Forget about your speedometer; it's not important. What is, is how many revs you are turning. That should be your concern, not your top speed. Of all your instruments your tach is the most important and should be checked at every up-shift. The other instruments need only be checked two or three times a lap—but be sure to do it. It's best to pick a couple spots on longish straight-aways to give them a quick glance. That quick glance at your oil pressure

*Choose a couple of spots on each lap to quickly check all your gauges . . . The banking at Daytona is an example of a good spot; just cruisin' along at about 200-plus, not much else to do but read the needles.*

and water temperature gauges will let you know if you have problems on the way. They can save you a lot of money, so use them.

Don't spend too many laps on the track without a break or you'll find yourself making the same mistakes time after time. Eight to ten laps are usually a good number to run at one time. Then, come in and figure out what you've been doing right or wrong. Get out of the car and really think about it. Isolate what you did right and what you did wrong; find ways to improve when you go out again. Isolate where you could be smoother, faster, more consistent. Did you hit your apex areas right? How about your down-shifts? Are you trail-braking properly? Is your chassis set properly through the turns? Did you really blow a couple of turns? Are you braking late enough? Your perspective changes once you've stepped out of the car. That's the time to think about it, not when you're driving around at speed. All that will do is break your concentration and you'll screw-up somewhere else. If you make a mistake, correct it as best you can smoothly, then put it aside till you've finished that session. When behind the wheel, think about where you are going, not where you've been.

One word about practicing braking. Most novice drivers don't realize how deep they can brake into a corner in a race car. This is something that you must learn. The best way to practice this is to find a hard, ninety-degree corner or hairpin with a lot of

The information from section timing is valuable data that clearly shows the worth of modifications to your car or your technique.

run-off room where a spin would not be dangerous. Each time you approach the turn try braking a little later and a little later until you reach a point where either you don't gain anything or you spin. When you practice your braking, don't forget the basics: lightly double-pump, then squeeze on your brake pedal so you can feel what the brakes are doing, trail-brake into the first part of the turn, slowly easing off to keep your chassis set and then ease on the throttle. It's simple, once you know how deep you can go into one turn, you should be able to figure out other turns without looping it. Don't forget to try alternate lines on some turns just to see what will happen if you are forced to use them under racing conditions. No matter what you work at to improve, do it completely and methodically with full concentration. You'll increase your confidence as well as your ability. Your marked progress will definitely help you to build enthusiasm and self assurance.

If you have some friends who can give you a hand on your test days and at the races, they can help you make better use of your time by video-taping and section timing. Just as pro football players review their game tapes, a video system will give you the benefit of being able to see, on the spot, the replay of what you did right and what you did wrong. From reviewing these tapes you can immediately begin working on the problems. Having a friend time you through specific corners or sections as you experiment with variations in line, braking or other techniques can be useful also. Even though you may have the same tach reading at the exit of a turn, one line might be slightly quicker than another. With section timing this can be readily seen.

You could also film, tape and time your competition in the same sections as you do yourself, then compare. It'll help you come closer to them by seeing what they do right or wrong as compared to yourself. The better you know your competition the better you'll do against them.

Another thing, please try not to be a dry weather driver. If it is raining, go for it anyway. Lots of drivers pack up and leave for home at the first sight of rain. Practice is practice. Road races are also run in the rain so you'd better practice in the rain, too, if you want to get good at it. Besides, driving in the wet is a fantastic way to practice. You have to be smoother, gentler, concentrate harder and be even more precise at controlling your car. At a much slower speed you can experience less traction and faster responses from your car. The wet track forces you to be a better driver; so take advantage of the rain and practice, you'll be amazed how much you can learn. You'll end up being quicker in the dry from it, too.

As far as practice goes, it goes for all time. Every time you're behind the wheel, practice—on street or track. Like I said before, use your head, be careful, don't jeopardize anyone else and take it easy on the street. Driving on the street is a good place to practice

*You can learn a lot from practicing in the rain. Wet conditions are a fact of life in this sport, especially in England. Here I am in Sid Taylor's McLaren at Silverstone in '66. I finished second behind Denny Hulme.*

*smoothness, concentration, shifting, heel-and-toe and other basic techniques that you'll need on the racetrack. If you practice and perfect them while on the street, then when you're on the track you can concentrate on other aspects of racing, like testing.*

*Testing is practice, true. But, although you're combining all the basics you've learned from practice, you are also now starting to experiment and develop your car. You've got yourself dialed in, now it's time for your car.*

*RULE #1. . .(this one's the most important)* only change one thing at a time!

*RULE #2. . .record each change made and its effect.*

*RULE #3. . .time every lap. (always, practice and testing)*

*RULE #4. . .keep records for each circuit.*

*All this should save you time and make your testing more productive. Try to be able to test at a session apart from a race meet. You'll have more time and be more efficient. Then, when it comes to race qualifying you'll do better.*

*A word about Rule #1: If you have a handling problem, take each change as a separate thing. It may be your tire pressure, your shock absorber adjustment or anti-roll bar adjustment. Just change one thing at a time. Find out if it makes it better or worse before you make another change. Record each effect then move on to the next change, and work that out. It's a process of elimination. Do it orderly, for the best results.*

*Maybe your problem isn't even mechanical, maybe it's you or what you're doing. Some problems are really solved simply. Use your head and run your eight or ten laps, then get out and think about what you've been doing. A Corvette driver I knew was having trouble with his brakes one weekend. It was an important national race and he was really under pressure to do well. But, he wasn't thinking. He reported his brakes were pulling hard to the right at the end of two long and fast straights. His crew couldn't find anything wrong, but tried like hell to correct the problem. It wasn't the brakes. . .it was him. He was pushing so hard on the brakes to slow the big Vette that he was accidentally pulling up on the steering wheel for leverage. The car wasn't pulling to the right under braking; it was being steered unconsciously to the right. Every move you make behind the wheel affects what your car does. Use your head; think and you'll do all right.*

*Whatever your racing choice, it takes a lot of time behind the wheel to perfect it. Give a lot of thought to the kinds of racing available to you. They're all good practice. Go-karts, midgets, sprints, stockers—all of them will give you experience and that's what's necessary when you're starting. A lot of the current Formula One drivers started in go-karts. It's fast and competitive and, like motorcycles, it teaches you to get used to having competitors close around you. Whatever you can drive on a track is better than not driving at all. Practice with them the same as you would in a real racer. Do eight or ten laps then get out and think about it. When you do your next five or ten laps a few minutes later you'll be quicker.*

*Well, you're just about on your own now. I hope you listened and think about what you're doing. Take your time and do it right. Practice to perfect it and read, read, read. Read everything you can about racing, car preparation and the rules. Read the classified ads as well as the auto and racing publications. Everything has clues—learn to read and interpret them. Give yourself a broad base of knowledge and you'll have a lot more to draw from.*

*In our final section on sources you'll get a full list of recommended reading, schools and publications as well as some companies that can provide you with good information on what they are doing for racing and for you.*

*I hope you're getting along ok. You've got your national SCCA license and you're on your way to qualifying for the national run-offs at Atlanta? Your training program sounds both rigorous and a lot of fun. You love driving a great car at the limit; the best part is the start of the race and when you get the checker. Great to hear it.*

*How about your sponsors? You're salable. Fine, you've already lined up next season's sponsors. That's planning ahead. Sounds like you've really laid out your program and are sticking to it. Formula racing next year. Better, more competitive and if you do well a lot more people will notice you. You've done well this season. You really listened and got it dialed in. I wish all of my students were so attentive. You know, if you keep up the good work, you might even make the history books. You never know. You really have all it takes: talent, brains, quick reactions, good physical condition and a way of attracting sponsorship. . .not to mention you are really fast and good at driving. Who knows, you're young enough, you might be just the one to go on and become the first woman to win a World Championship Grand Prix (if Desiré Wilson doesn't beat you to it).*

*Now's the time to decide if you really want to make racing a career. If you think you might, let's work out a long- and short-term plan to get you headed in the right direction. The best of luck to you and keep in touch. See you at the races.*

*See you at the races!*

# SOURCES

## Driving Schools

Bob Bondurant School of High Performance Driving
Sears Point International Raceway
Highways 37 and 121
Sonoma, California 95476
Telephone (707) 938-4741

Bertil Roos School of Motor Racing
Pocono International Raceway
Box 221-T
Blakeslee, Pennsylvania 18610
Telephone (717) 646-7227 or
646-3174

Bill Scott Racing School
P.O. Box 190
Summit Point, West Virginia 25446
Telephone (304) 725-4071

Skip Barber Racing School
1000 Massachusetts Avenue
Boxboro, Massachusetts 01719
Telephone (617) 263-3771

British School of Motor Racing
Riverside International Raceway
22255 Eucalyptus Avenue
Riverside, California 92508
Telephone (714) 656-3576
British School also located at Laguna
Seca International Raceway.

Jim Russell International Racing
Drivers School, Canada
Box 119-AC9
Mt. Tremblant, Quebec J0T 1Z0
Canada
Telephone (819) 425-2739

## Publications

AUTOCAR
Quadrant House
The Quadrant
Sutton, Surrey
England SM25AS

AUTOSPORT
38-42 Hampton Road
Teddington, Middlesex
England

AUTOWEEK
965 East Jefferson
Detroit, Michigan 48207

CAR AND DRIVER
2002 Hogback Road
Ann Arbor, Michigan 48104

GRAND PRIX INTERNATIONAL
(North American English Edition)
Long Beach Grand Prix Association
110 W. Ocean Suite A
Long Beach, California 90802

MOTOR
IPC Business Press Ltd.
Surrey House
1 Throwley Way
Sutton, Surrey
England SM1 4QQ

MOTORING NEWS
Standard House
Bonhill Street
London
England ECZA 4DA

MOTOR SPORT
Standard House
Bonhill Street
London
England ECZA 4DA

MOTOR TREND
HOT ROD
Petersen Publishing Company
8490 Sunset Blvd.
Los Angeles, California 90069

ON TRACK
3629 West Warner Ave.
Santa Ana, California 92704

ROAD & TRACK
1499 Monrovia Avenue
Newport Beach, California 92663

## Sanctioning Bodies

ACCUS (Automobile Competition
Committee for the United States)
F.I.A. (Federation Internationale de
l'Automobile)
1701 "K" Street N.W. Suite 1204
Washington D.C. 20006
Telephone (202) 833-9133

CART (Championship Auto Racing
Teams)
3221 West Big Beaver Road Suite 205
Troy, Michigan 48084
Telephone (313) 643-6440

IMSA (International Motor Sports
Association)
P.O. Box 3465
Bridgeport, Connecticut 06605
Telephone (203) 336-2116

NASCAR (National Association of
Stock Car Auto Racing)
P.O. Box K
Daytona, Florida 32015

SCCA (Sports Car Club of America)
P.O. Box 3278
6750 South Emporia
Englewood, Colorado 80112
Telephone (303) 770-1044

USAC (United States Auto Club)
4910 West 16th St.
Indianapolis, Indiana 46224

## Books

*All But My Life*
Sterling Moss and Ken Purdy
William Kimber & Co.
London England, 1963

*Autocourse* (Annual)
U.S. Distributor
Motorbooks International
Osceola, Wisconsin 54020

*F.I.A. Yearbook* (Annual)
Federation Internationale de l'Automobile
8 Place de la Concorde
75008 Paris, France

*Formula Car Technology*
Howdy Holmes
Steve Smith Autosports Publications
Santa Ana, California, 1980

*Prepare To Win*
Carroll Smith
Aero Publishers, Inc.
Fallbrook, California, 1975

*Racing Car Design and Development*
Len Terry and Alan Baker
Robert Bentley, Inc.
Cambridge, Massachusetts, 1973

*The Art and Science of Grand Prix
Driving*
Niki Lauda
Motorbooks International
Osceola, Wisconsin, 1977

*The Racing Driver, The Theory and
Practice of Fast Driving*
Denis Jenkinson
Robert Bentley Inc.
Cambridge, Massachusetts, 1958

*The Technique of Motor Racing*
Piero Taruffi
Robert Bentley, Inc.
Cambridge, Massachusetts, 1958

*The Unfair Advantage*
Mark Donohue
Dodd, Mead & Co.
New York, New York, 1975

*Tune To Win*
Carroll Smith
Aero Publishers, Inc.
Fallbrook, California, 1978

## Miscellaneous Sources

Bandag Racing Retreads
Bandag, Inc.
1056 Hershey Ave.
Muscatine, Iowa 52761

Bell Helmets
15301 Shoemaker Ave.
Norwalk, California 90650

Center Line Wheels
13521 Preeway Drive
Santa Fe Springs, California 90670

Classic Motorbooks (literature)
P.O. Box 1
Osceola, Wisconsin 54020

Kontrolle Shocks
4445 Enterprise St.
Fremont, California 94539

Quickor Suspension Systems
6710 Southwest 111th
Beaverton, Oregon 97005

RaceMark Driving Suits
RaceMark Manufacturing
P.O. Box 1089
Schenectady, New York 12301

Recaro Seats
Recaro U.S.A.
1152 E. Dominguez St.
Carson, California 90745

Safety Devices, Inc., U.S.A. (Roll bars)
15 Central Way
Department 300
Kirkland, Washington 98033

Simpson Safety Equipment
22630 So. Normandie Ave.
Torrance, California 90502

# More Great Reading

**Illustrated Ferrari Buyer's Guide.** Features all street/production cars 1954 through 1980. 176 pages, over 225 photos, softbound.

**Illustrated Porsche Buyer's Guide.** Covers the 356 through the 944 from 1950 to 1983 with lots of photos. Softbound, 175 pages.

**Ferrari Dino 206GT, 246GT & GTS.** These Pininfarina-designed V-6 Ferraris with bodies by Scaglietti are covered with 90 illustrations, 12 in color. 137 pages, in the AutoHistory series.

**Illustrated Mercedes-Benz Buyer's Guide.** Thorough coverage of models through 1983 with lots of photos. Softbound, 175 pages.

**Porsche 924, 928, 944: The New Generation.** Detailed development story of these front-engined Porsches 1975-1981. 136 pages, 90 illustrations, 8 pages of color.

**Ferrari 275GTB & GTS.** The 2-cam, 4-cam Competizione and Spider are covered in this AutoHistory series volume. 90 illustrations, some in color, 136 pages.

**Legend of the Lotus Seven.** Definitive book on this classic Lotus. Story is covered thoroughly in 224 pages with 150 illustrations.

**Lamborghini: The Cars From Sant'Agata Bolognese.** Through 1981 covers design and technical features of the cars with a model-by-model guide of over 300 photos, some in color. 208 pages.

**Mercedes-Benz V8s.** Covers the sedans and limousines from 1963, including 600, 350, 450 and 500 series. 136 pages with 80 photos, 12 in color.

**Porsche 356.** In the AutoHistory series. Models included are: Coupe, Cabriolet, Roadster, Speedster and Carrera. Great introductory reading. 136 pages, 80 illustrations plus 8 pages of color.

**Mini-Cooper and S.** In the AutoHistory series. Models covered are: 997 and 998 Cooper; 970, 1071 and 1275 S. 136 pages, 92 photos including 12 in color.

**Jaguar E-Type.** This AutoHistory series volume covers the 3.8 and 4.2 6-cylinders plus the 5.3 V-12. 80 photos plus 8 pages of color, 136 pages.

**Ford Escort RS.** In the AutoHistory series. Models covered are: Twin-Cam; RS 1600, 1800, 2000; Mexico. 136 pages, 92 illustrations, including 12 in color.

**Jaguar XJ.** The 6 and 12, Daimler, Vanden Plas and XJ-S are covered in this volume of the AutoHistory series. 136 pages, 80 illustrations plus 12 in color.

**Aston Martin V8's.** In the AutoHistory series. Covers the DBS V-8, V-8, Vantage, Volante, Lagonda and Bulldog. 80 illustrations plus 12 in color, 128 pages.

**Citroen SM.** Covers these 2.7-liter V-6 Maserati-engined cars. 91 illustrations accompany this thorough introduction. 128 pages, in the AutoHistory series.

**Ferrari Berlinetta Boxer.** Includes the 365 and 512 series. In the AutoHistory series. 80 photos plus 12 in color, 136 pages.

**Lamborghini Countach.** Covers LP500, LP400, Countach & S, and V-12 mid-engined rare, exotic Italian models. 136 pages, 92 illustrations with 12 in color.

**De Tomaso Pantera.** In the AutoHistory series. Includes thorough introduction information on the 351 V-8, L, GTS, GR3 and GT4. 92 photos including 12 in color, 136 pages.

**Porsche 911 Turbo.** Covers the life and times of the 3- and 3.3-liter models including production and racing careers. 136 pages, 92 illustrations including 8 pages of color. In the AutoHistory series.